English Grammar for the Utterly Confused

Laurie Rozakis, Ph.D.

McGraw-Hill

New York   Chicago   San Francisco   Lisbon   London   Madrid
Mexico City   Milan   New Delhi   San Juan   Seoul   Singapore
Sydney   Toronto

The McGraw·Hill Companies

1 2 3 4 5 6 7 8 9 10 11   DOC/DOC   0 9 8 7 6 5 4 3

ISBN 0-07-139922-4

McGraw-Hill books are available at special quantity discounts to use as premiums and
sales promotions, or for use in corporate training programs. For more information, please
write to the Director of Special Sales, McGraw-Hill, Two Penn Plaza, New York, NY
10121. Or contact your local bookstore.

 This book is printed on recycled, acid-free paper containing a minimum of 50%
recycled, de-inked fiber.

To Robert from Farmingdale . . . always and forever.

Acknowledgments

I would like to thank Barbara Gilson, the editorial director of McGraw-Hill. Barbara, you are a dear friend, and it is always a treat working with you.

Thank you also to all the hard-working people at McGraw-Hill who take my manuscripts and turn them into books. They are Andrew Littell, Maureen B. Walker, and Maureen Harper. You make me look so good!

And grateful acknowledgement to the wonderful staff of the Farmingdale Public Library. From reference to circulation, youth services to technical processing, you always manage to get me the material I need. Your experience, expertise, and kindness are much appreciated. Finally, my thanks to my children, Charles and Samantha, and their friends. When "book writing" gets tough, I can always count on the kids for a much-needed break!

Contents

Preface

I have the world's nicest students. They are polite, earnest, and sweet. They are fun to talk to and a delight to teach. Unfortunately, many of them are ill-prepared for college. They are not ready for the onslaught of work and do not know how to write. Many have not been taught grammar, usage, or mechanics.

After interviewing students across the country—including many at the nation's top schools—I have come to realize that this dilemma is not unique to my students. Far from it. Worst of all, a distressing number of students believe they cannot succeed. They have been shaken by years of low grades or grade inflation that results in artificially-raised scores.

This book is designed to help *all* students master the basics of English grammar that they need to succeed in their studies. Best of all, when students understand the underpinnings of our language, learning will be fun—as it should be.

—LAURIE ROZAKIS, PH.D.
FARMINGDALE STATE COLLEGE

Organization of the Text

This book is arranged in five sections for a total of fourteen chapters. The chapters take you step-by-step through the process of learning English grammar and usage. Each chapter ends with a series of review exercises. These help you reinforce and extend what you learned. The exercises include true-false, completion, and multiple-choice test items.

Here's how to use this book:

Option 1
- Read through the book from the beginning to the end as you would any book.
- Complete all the exercises at the end of each chapter to assess your progress. This gives you even more practice with grammar.

Option 2
- Pick and choose the chapters you wish to read, or read them in any order you like.
- Skim the exercises to find the ones that help you learn more about the areas in which you need improvement.

Option 3
- Use the book as a study guide right before and after major tests. Read and reread the chapters you need the most.
- Complete the exercises that directly match the types of tests you are taking now or plan to take in the immediate future.

◆◆◆◆◆◆◆◆◆◆◆◆◆◆◆◆◆◆◆◆◆◆◆◆◆◆◆◆◆◆◆◆◆◆◆◆

PART 1

CHAPTER 1

Parts of Speech

◆◆◆◆◆◆◆◆◆◆◆◆◆◆◆◆◆◆◆◆◆◆◆◆◆◆◆◆◆◆◆◆◆◆◆◆

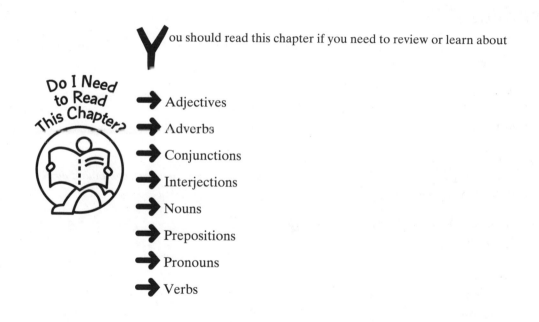

Y ou should read this chapter if you need to review or learn about

Do I Need to Read This Chapter?

➜ Adjectives

➜ Adverbs

➜ Conjunctions

➜ Interjections

➜ Nouns

➜ Prepositions

➜ Pronouns

➜ Verbs

In this chapter, you'll review parts of speech so that you have a standard way to describe how words are put together to create meaning. The parts of speech are arranged in alphabetical order for easy reference. In later chapters, you will learn how to correct errors caused by misusing these parts of speech.

◆◆

Get Started

English is a very flexible language. A word's meaning is derived not only from how it is spelled and pronounced but also from how it is used in a sentence. As you review the parts of speech, remember that *the way a word is used in a sentence determines which part of speech it is.* For example:

Noun: I ate a *fish* for dinner.

Verb: We *fish* in the lake on every Tuesday.

Adjectives

Adjectives are words that describe nouns and pronouns. Adjectives answer the questions: *What kind? How much? Which one? How many?* For example:

What kind?	*red* nose	*gold* ring
How much?	*more* sugar	*little* effort
Which one?	*second* chance	*those* chocolates
How many?	*several* chances	*six* books

There are five kinds of adjectives: *common adjectives, proper adjectives, compound adjectives, articles,* and *indefinite adjectives*.

1. *Common adjectives* describe nouns or pronouns.
   strong man
   green plant
   beautiful view

2. *Proper adjectives* are formed from proper nouns.
   California vegetables (from the noun "California")
   Mexican food (from the noun "Mexico")

3. *Compound adjectives* are made up of more than one word.
   far-off country
   teenage person

4. *Articles* are a special type of adjective. There are three articles: *a, an, the.*
   The is called a "definite article" because it refers to a specific thing.
   A and *an* are called "indefinite articles" because they refer to general things. Use *a* with consonant sounds; use *an* before vowel sounds.

5. *Indefinite adjectives* don't specify the specific amount of something.

all	another	any	both
each	either	few	many
more	most	neither	other
several	some		

Follow these guidelines when you use adjectives:

1. Use an adjective to describe a noun or a pronoun.
   Jesse was *unwilling* to leave *the* circus.
   noun   adj.   adj. noun

2. Use vivid adjectives to make your writing more specific and descriptive.
   Take a *larger* slice of the *luscious* cake.
         adj.   noun   adj.   noun

3. Use an adjective after a linking verb. A linking verb connects a subject with a descriptive word. The most common linking verbs are *be* (*is, am, are, was, were,* and so on), *seem, appear, look, feel, smell, sound, taste, become, grow, remain, stay,* and *turn.*
   Chicken made this way *tastes* more *delicious* (not *deliciously*).

Quick Tip

Predicate adjectives are adjectives separated from the noun or pronoun by a linking verb. Predicate adjectives describe the subject of the sentence.

The weather was *cold* all week.

Adverbs

Adverbs are words that describe verbs, adjectives, or other adverbs. Adverbs answer the questions: *When? Where? How?* or *To what extent?*

When?	left yesterday	begin now
Where?	fell below	move up
How?	happily sang	danced badly
To what extent?	partly finished	eat completely

Most adverbs are formed by adding *-ly* to an adjective. For example:

Adjective		Adverb
Quick	—	quickly
Careful	—	carefully
Accurate	—	accurately

Here are some of the most common non-*ly* adverbs:

afterward	almost	already	also	back	even
far	fast	hard	here	how	late
long	low	more	near	never	next
now	often	quick	rather	slow	soon
still	then	today	tomorrow	too	when
where	yesterday				

Follow these guidelines when you use adverbs:

1. Use an adverb to describe a verb.
   Experiments using dynamite must be done *carefully*.
                                        verb   adv.

2. Use an adverb to describe an adjective.
   Sam had an *unbelievably huge* appetite for chips.
                     adv.   adj.

3. Use an adverb to describe another adverb.
   They sang *so clearly*.
             adv. adv.

Quick Tip

Conjunctive adverbs are used to connect other words and to link ideas and paragraphs.

accordingly	again	also	besides
consequently	finally	for example	furthermore
however	indeed	moreover	on the other hand
otherwise	nevertheless	then	therefore

Conjunctions

Conjunctions connect words or groups of words and show how the words are related. There are three kinds of conjunctions: *coordinating conjunctions, correlative conjunctions,* and *subordinating conjunctions.*

1. *Coordinating conjunctions* link similar words or word groups. There are seven coordinating conjunctions:

   for   and   nor   but   or   yet   so

Quick Tip

Use this mnemonic to help you remember the seven coordinating conjunctions: *FANBOYS* (*for, and, nor, but, or, yet, so*).

---

2. *Correlative conjunctions* also link similar words or word groups, but they are always used in pairs. Here are the correlative conjunctions:

   both . . .and   either . . . or
   neither . . . nor   not only . . . but also   whether . . . or

3. *Subordinating conjunctions* link an independent clause (complete sentence) to a dependent clause (fragment). Here are the most often used subordinating conjunctions:

after	although	as	as if
as long as	as soon as	as though	because
before	even though	if	in order that
since	so that	though	till
unless	until	when	whenever
where	wherever		

Interjections

Interjections show strong emotion. Since interjections are not linked grammatically to other words in the sentence, they are set off from the rest of the sentence with a comma or an exclamation mark. For example:

- *Oh!* What a shock you gave me with that gorilla suit.
- *Wow!* That's not a gorilla suit!

Nouns

A *noun* is a word that names a person, place, or thing. Nouns come in these varieties: *common nouns, proper nouns, compound nouns,* and *collective nouns.*

1. *Common nouns* name any one of a class of person, place, or thing.
   girl   city   food
2. *Proper nouns* name a specific person, place, or thing. Proper nouns are always capitalized.
   Barbara   New York City   Rice-a-Roni
3. *Compound nouns* are two or more nouns that function as a single unit. A compound noun can be two individual words, words joined by a hyphen, or two words combined.
   Individual words: time capsule
   Hyphenated words: great-uncle
   Combined words: basketball
4. *Collective nouns* name groups of people or things.
   audience   family   herd   crowd

Possessive Nouns

In grammar, *possession* shows ownership. Follow these rules to create possessive nouns.

1. With singular nouns, add an apostrophe and an *s.*
   dog → dog's bone
   singer → singer's voice
2. With plural nouns ending in *s,* add an apostrophe after the *s.*
   dogs → dogs' bones
   singers → singers' voices
3. With plural nouns not ending in *s,* add an apostrophe and an *s.*
   men → men's books
   mice → mice's tails

Plural Nouns

Here are the guidelines for creating plural nouns.

1. Add *s* to form the plural of most nouns.
   cat → cats   computer → computers
2. Add *es* if the noun ends in *s, sh, ch,* or *x.*
   wish → wishes   inch → inches   box → boxes

3. If a noun ends in consonant -*y,* change the *y* to *i* and add *es.*
   city → cities   lady → ladies

4. If a noun ends in vowel -*y,* add *s.* Words ending in -*quy* don't follow this rule (as in *soliloquies*).
   essay → essays   monkey → monkeys

Prepositions

Prepositions link a noun or a pronoun following it to another word in the sentence. Use this chart to help you recognize some of the most common prepositions:

about	above	across	after	against	along
amid	around	as	at	before	behind
below	beneath	beside	between	beyond	but
by	despite	down	during	except	for
from	in	inside	into	like	near
on	onto	of	off	opposite	out
outside	over	past	since	through	to
toward	under	underneath	until	upon	with

A noun or pronoun always follows a preposition. A *prepositional phrase* is a preposition and its object. A prepositional phrase can be two or three words long.

> *on the wing*   *in the door*

However, prepositional phrases also can be much longer, depending on the length of the preposition and the number of words that describe the object of the preposition.

> *near* the violently swaying oak trees

> *on account of* his nearly depleted bank account

Pronouns

A *pronoun* is a word used in place of a noun or another pronoun. Pronouns help you avoid unnecessary repetition in your writing and speech. A pronoun gets its meaning from the noun it stands for. The noun is called the *antecedent.*

> Although *Seattle* is damp, *it* is my favorite city.
>   antecedent   pronoun

There are different kinds of pronouns. Most of them have antecedents, but a few do not.

STOP

Quick Tip

The word *antecedent* comes from a Latin word meaning "to go before." However, the noun does not have to appear before the pronoun in a sentence. It often does, though, to keep sentences clear and avoid misreadings.

---

1. *Personal pronouns* refer to a specific person, place, object, or thing.

	Singular	Plural
First person	I, me, mine, my	we, us, our, ours
Second person	you, your, yours	you, your, yours
Third person	he, him, his, she, her, hers, it	they, them, their, theirs, its

2. *Possessive pronouns* show ownership. The possessive pronouns are: *your, yours, his, hers, its, ours, their, theirs, whose.*
   Is this beautiful plant *yours?*
   Yes, it's *ours.*

Quick Tip

Don't confuse personal pronouns with contractions. Personal pronouns never have an apostrophe, while contractions always have an apostrophe. Use this chart:

Pronoun	Contraction
yours	you're (you are)
its	it's (it is)
their	they're (they are)
whose	who's (who is)

---

3. *Reflexive pronouns* add information to a sentence by pointing back to a noun or pronoun near the beginning of the sentence. Reflexive pronouns end in *-self* or *-selves*.

Tricia bought *herself* a new car.

All her friends enjoyed *themselves* riding in the beautiful car.

4. *Intensive pronouns* also end in *-self* or *-selves* but just add emphasis to the noun or pronoun.

Tricia *herself* picked out the car.

5. *Demonstrative pronouns* direct attention to a specific person, place, or thing. There are only four demonstrative pronouns: *this, that, these, those.*

This is my favorite movie.

That was a fierce rain storm.

6. *Relative pronouns* begin a subordinate clause. There are five relative pronouns: *that, which, who, whom, those.*

Jasper claimed *that* he could run the washing machine.

Louise was the repair person *who* fixed the machine after Jasper washed his sneakers.

Singular	Plural	Singular or Plural
another	both	all
anyone	few	any
each	many	more
everyone	others	most
everybody	several	none
everything		some
much		
nobody		
nothing		
other		
someone		
anybody		
anything		
either		
little		
neither		
no one		
one		
somebody		
something		

7. *Interrogative pronouns* ask a question. They are: *what, which, who, whom, whose.*
    Who would like to cook dinner?
    Which side does the fork go on?

8. *Indefinite pronouns* refer to people, places, objects, or things without pointing to a specific one. The most common indefinite pronouns are listed in the chart on the previous page.

Verbs

Verbs name an action or describe a state of being. Every sentence must have a verb. There are three basic types of verbs: *action verbs, linking verbs,* and *helping verbs.*

Action Verbs

Action verbs tell what the subject does. The action can be visible (*jump, kiss, laugh*) or mental (*think, learn, study*).

The cat *broke* Louise's china.

Louise *considered* buying a new china cabinet.

An action verb can be *transitive* or *intransitive. Transitive verbs* need a direct object.

The boss *dropped* the ball.

The workers *picked* it up.

Intransitive verbs do not need a direct object.

Who *called?*

The temperature *fell* over night.

Quick Tip

To determine if a verb is transitive, ask yourself "Who?" or "What?" after the verb. If you can find an answer in the sentence, the verb is transitive.

Linking Verbs

Linking verbs join the subject and the predicate. They do not show action. Instead, they help the words at the end of the sentence name or describe the subject. As you read earlier in this chapter, the most common linking verbs include: *be, feel, grow, seem, smell, remain, appear, sound, stay, look, taste, turn, become.* Look for forms of *to be*, such as *am, are, is, was, were, am being, can be, have been*, and so on.

The manager *was* happy about the job change.

He *is* a good worker.

Many linking verbs can also be used as action verbs.

Linking: The kids *looked* sad.

Action: I *looked* for the dog in the pouring rain.

Quick Tip

To determine whether a verb is being used as a linking verb or an action verb, substitute *am, are,* or *is* for the verb. If it makes sense, the original verb is a linking verb.

Helping Verbs

Helping verbs are added to another verb to make the meaning clearer. Helping verbs include any form of *to be, do, does, did, have, has, had, shall, should, will, would, can, could, may, might, must. Verb phrases* are made up of one main verb and one or more helping verbs.

They *will run* before dawn.

They *still have not yet found* a smooth track.

English has eight parts of speech:

✔ Adjectives

✔ Adverbs

✔ Conjunctions

✔ Interjections

✔ Nouns

✔ Prepositions

Pronouns

 Verbs

The way a word is used in a sentence determines what part of speech it is.

QUESTIONS

True-False Questions

1. A noun names a person, place, or thing.

2. Common nouns name any one of a class of person, place, or thing.

3. Proper nouns name a specific person, place, or thing. Proper nouns are never capitalized.

4. Plural nouns show ownership.

5. Verbs express action, condition, or state of being.

6. There are six basic types of verbs: action verbs, linking verbs, helping verbs, transitive verbs, intransitive verbs, and plural verbs.

7. Helping verbs are added to another verb to make the meaning clearer. Helping verbs include any form of *to be.*

8. Adjectives describe nouns and pronouns.

9. Never use an adjective after a linking verb.

10. Adverbs describe verbs, adjectives, or other adverbs.

11. All adverbs are formed by adding *-ly* to an adjective.

12. Prepositions link a verb to another word.

13. A pronoun gets its meaning from the noun it stands for. The noun is called the *antecedent.*

14. Conjunctions connect words or groups of words.

15. Interjections express strong emotions and are usually set off with an exclamation mark (!).

Completion Questions

Select the word that best completes each sentence.

1. Proper adjectives are formed from (common nouns, proper nouns).

2. The three articles are *a, an,* and (*the, then*).

3. *The* is called the (indefinite article, definite article).

4. (Predicate adjectives, Proper adjectives), which describe the subject of the sentence, are adjectives separated from the noun or pronoun by a linking verb.

5. (Interjections, Conjunctive adverbs) are used to connect other words and to link ideas and paragraphs.

6. There are (three, seven) different coordinating conjunctions.

7. Correlative conjunctions also link similar words or word groups, but they are always used (in pairs, one at a time).

8. Collective nouns (name groups, show ownership).

9. (I, Which) is a personal pronoun.

10. (Yours, Herself) is a possessive pronoun.

11. Intensive pronouns, unlike reflexive pronouns, (begin a subordinate clause, add emphasis).

12. (Interrogative pronouns, Indefinite pronouns) ask a question. They are: *what, which, who, whom, whose.*

13. Every sentence must have a noun and a (preposition, verb).

14. Action verbs can be visible and (mental, linking).

15. In the sentence "Luis dropped his hat," the verb *dropped* is (transitive, intransitive)

16. In the sentence "Nita awoke early," the verb *awoke* is (transitive, intransitive).

17. To determine if a verb is transitive, ask yourself ("Who?"/"What?", "How many?") after the verb.

18. (Helping verbs, Linking verbs) join the subject and the predicate and do not show action.

19. Helping verbs, which are added to another verb to make the meaning clearer, can include any form of (to be, to see).

20. In the sentence "I traded my sandwich for three oatmeal cookies," the word *oatmeal* is a/n (noun, adjective).

Multiple-Choice Questions

Identify the part of speech for the underlined word in each sentence.

1. The <u>outside</u> of the boat needs scraping.
   - (a) Noun
   - (b) Adjective
   - (c) Adverb
   - (d) Preposition

2. You should scrape the boat without <u>outside</u> help.
   - (a) Noun
   - (b) Adjective
   - (c) Adverb
   - (d) Preposition

3. Let's sit <u>outside</u> and laugh at you as you work in the blazing sun.
    (a) Noun
    (b) Adjective
    (c) Adverb
    (d) Preposition

4. The ambulance is parked right <u>outside</u> the yard, next to the beehive.
    (a) Noun
    (b) Adjective
    (c) Adverb
    (d) Preposition

5. The politician repented of his <u>past</u> mistakes.
    (a) Noun
    (b) Adjective
    (c) Adverb
    (d) Preposition

6. Turn right <u>past</u> the store with the neon sign in the window.
    (a) Noun
    (b) Adjective
    (c) Adverb
    (d) Preposition

7. Did you hear that song <u>before?</u>
    (a) Conjunction
    (b) Adjective
    (c) Adverb
    (d) Preposition

8. Always follow <u>through with</u> what you start.
    (a) Interjection
    (b) Conjunction
    (c) Adverb
    (d) Preposition

9. The remark went right <u>through</u> one ear and out the other.
    (a) Noun
    (b) Adjective
    (c) Conjunction
    (d) Preposition

10. The gardener mowed the lawn <u>after</u> he reread *Lady Chatterly's Lover.*
    (a) Conjunction
    (b) Adjective

      (c) Adverb

      (d) Preposition

ANSWER KEY

True-False Questions

1. T   2. T   3. F   4. F   5. T   6. F   7. T   8. T   9. F   10. T   11. F   12. F
13. T   14. T   15. T

Completion Questions

1. proper nouns   2. the   3. definite article   4. Predicate adjectives   5. Conjunctive adverbs   6. seven   7. in pairs   8. name groups   9. I   10. Yours   11. add emphasis   12. Interrogative pronouns   13. verb   14. mental   15. transitive
16. intransitive   17. "Who?"/"What?"   18. Linking verbs   19. to be   20. adjective

Multiple-Choice Questions

1. a   2. b   3. c   4. d   5. b   6. d   7. c   8. c   9. d   10. a

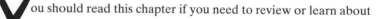

CHAPTER 2

Using Pronouns Correctly

Y ou should read this chapter if you need to review or learn about

➡ Understanding *case,* the form of a pronoun that shows how it is used in a sentence

➡ Using personal pronouns correctly

➡ Correcting pronoun reference

➡ Revising sexist pronoun reference

➡ Using *who, which, that*

Get Started

You'll recall from Chapter 1 that a *pronoun* is a word used in place of a noun or another pronoun. A pronoun gets its meaning from the noun it replaces, called the *antecedent.*

    Case refers to the form of a noun or pronoun that shows how it is used in a sentence.

Overview of Pronoun Case

Only two parts of speech, nouns and pronouns, have *case*. This means that they change form depending on how they are used in a sentence. English has three cases: *nominative, objective,* and *possessive.*

- In the *nominative* case, the pronoun is used as a subject.
  I threw the ball.
- In the *objective* case, the pronoun is used as an object.
  Give the ball to *me.*
- In the *possessive* case, the pronoun is used to show ownership.
  The ball is *mine.*

The following chart shows the three cases of personal pronouns:

Nominative	Objective	Possessive
(Pronoun as subject)	(Pronoun as object)	(Ownership)
I	me	my, mine
you	you	your, yours
he	him	his
she	her	her, hers
it	it	its
we	us	our, ours
they	them	their, theirs
who	whom	whose
whoever	whomever	whoever

To avoid errors in personal pronoun use, you must understand how to use each case. The rules are explained below. Relax: They're actually not difficult at all!

Using the Nominative Case

1. Use the nominative case to show the subject of a verb.
   Father and (I, me) like to shop at flea markets.
   Answer: I is the subject of the sentence. Therefore, the pronoun is in the nominative case: "Father and *I* like to shop at flea markets."

   To help determine the correct pronoun, take away the first subject and try each choice. See which one sounds better. For example:

I like to shop at flea markets.
Me like to shop at flea markets.

The first one definitely sounds better.

Quick Tip

When you list two or more subjects, always put yourself last. Therefore, the sentence would read "Father and I," never "I and Father."

(Who, Whom) do you believe is the better shopper?
Answer: Who is the subject of the verb *is.* Therefore, the sentence would read, "*Who* do you believe is the better shopper?"

Ignore interrupting expressions such as *do you believe, you think, do you suppose* (and so on). They do not affect pronoun case.

2. Use the nominative case for a predicate nominative.

A *predicate nominative* is a noun or pronoun that follows a linking verb and identifies or renames the subject. Remember that a *linking verb* connects a subject to a word that renames it. *Linking verbs* indicate a state of being (*am, is, are,* etc.), relate to the senses (*look, smell, taste,* etc.), or indicate a condition (*appear, seem, become,* etc.).

The salesman of the month was (I, me).
Answer: Use *I,* since the pronoun renames the subject, the salesman of the month. "The salesman of the month was *I.*"

Which is correct: "It is *I*" or "It is *me*"? Technically, the correct form is "It is I," since we're dealing with a predicate nominative. However, "It is me" (and "It is us") has become increasingly acceptable as standard usage.

Using the Objective Case

1. Use the objective case to show a direct object.
A *direct object* is a noun or pronoun that receives the action.

John's suit no longer fits (he, him).
Answer: John's suit no longer fits *him.*

(Who, Whom) did she finally invite to the dinner party?
Answer: She is the subject, the person doing the action. Therefore, the sentence should read: "*Whom* did she finally invite to the dinner party?"

Of course, she can invite (whoever, whomever) she wants.
Answer: Of course, she can invite *whomever* she wants.

Quick Tip

When you have a pronoun combined with a noun (such as *we guests, us guests*), try the sentence without the noun. You can usually "hear" which pronoun sounds right.

It is always a pleasure for *we* to attend their party.

It is always a pleasure for *us* to attend their party.

The second sentence is correct.

---

2. Use the objective case to show an indirect object.

    An *indirect object* tells *to* or *for* whom something is done. You can tell a word is an indirect object if you can insert *to* or *for* before it without changing the meaning. For example: "The book gave (to) my boss and (to) me some new strategies."

    The bill gave (we, us) a shock.
    Answer: The bill gave *us* a shock.

3. Use the objective case for the object of a preposition.

    Remember that a preposition is a small word that links a noun or a pronoun following it to another word in the sentence.

    Sit by (I, me).
    Answer: The pronoun is the object of the preposition *me,* so the sentence reads: "Sit by *me.*"

Using the Possessive Case

1. Use the possessive case to show ownership.

    The child refused to admit that the sweater was (her's, hers).

    Answer: Hers is the correct spelling of the possessive case, which is needed here to express ownership (belonging to her). Therefore, the sentence should read: "The child refused to admit that the sweater was *hers.*"

2. Use the possessive case before gerunds.

    A *gerund* is a form of a verb that acts as a noun. Gerunds always end in *-ing,* and they always function as nouns.

    (You, Your) walking in the rain didn't cause your cold.

Answer: The gerund *walking* requires the possessive pronoun *your*. Therefore, the sentence should read: "*Your* walking in the rain didn't cause your cold."

Do you mind (my, me) borrowing your cell phone?

Answer: Do you mind *my* borrowing your cell phone?

3. Use some possessive pronouns alone to show ownership.

This cell phone is *mine,* not *yours.*

Three Other Rules for Using Pronouns

Here are three more rules that apply to pronouns and case.

1. A pronoun used in apposition with a noun is in the same case as the noun.

An *appositive phrase* is a noun or pronoun that adds information and details. Appositives can often be removed from the sentence, so they are set off with commas. The appositive in the following sentence is underlined.

Two police officers, <u>Alice and (she, her)</u>, were commended for bravery.

Answer: The pronoun must be in the nominative case (*she*) because it is in apposition with the noun *police officers,* which is in the nominative case. Therefore, the sentence should read: Two police officers, <u>Alice and *she*</u>, were commended for bravery.

Exception: *A pronoun used as the subject of an infinitive is in the objective case.* For example: "Juan expects Luz and (I, me) to host the reception." The correct pronoun here is *me,* since it is the subject of the infinitive *to host.*

Quick Tip

Pronouns that express ownership never get an apostrophe. Watch for these possessive pronouns: *yours, his, hers, its, ours, theirs.*

---

2. Use *-self* forms correctly with reflexive and intensive situations.

As you learned in Chapter 1, *reflexive pronouns* reflect back to the subject or object.

The child embarrassed *himself.*

Don't use reflexive pronouns in place of subjects and objects.

The boss and (myself, I) had a meeting.

Answer: Use the pronoun *I,* not the reflexive form. Therefore, the sentence reads: "The boss and *I* had a meeting."

3. *Who* is the nominative case; *whom* is the objective case.

No one will argue that *who* and *whom* are the most troublesome pronouns in English. Even though *who* and *whom* were discussed earlier in this chapter, these little words cause such distress that they deserve their own subsection. Let's start by looking back at our pronoun-use chart.

	Nominative	**Objective**	**Possessive**
	(Subject case)	(Object case)	(Ownership)
Singular	who	whom	whose
	whoever	whomever	whosoever
Plural	who	whom	whose
	whoever	whomever	whosoever

Now, some guidelines:

- Use *who* or *whoever* when the pronoun is the subject of a verb.
  Who won the Nobel Prize this year?

- Use *who* or *whoever* when the pronoun is the predicate nominative.
  The winner was *who?*

- Use *whom* or *whomever* when the pronoun is the direct object of a verb or the object of a preposition.
  Whom did he fire this week?

Use Correct Pronoun Reference

The meaning of a pronoun comes from its antecedent, the noun or pronoun to which it refers. Your speech and writing will be confusing if your pronoun reference is unclear.

Carelessly placed pronouns can create unintentionally funny sentences as well as confusing ones. Consider the difference between what the writer *thinks* he or she said and what is *really* being said in the following sentences:

Last week, a wart appeared on my right thumb, and I want *it* removed.
(Are you removing the wart or the thumb?)
Guilt and unkindness can be emotionally destructive to you and your friends. You must get rid of *them.*
(Are you getting rid of the guilt or your friends?)

There are three ways to prevent pronoun confusion.

1. A pronoun must clearly refer to a single antecedent.

2. Place pronouns close to their antecedents.

3. Make a pronoun refer to a definite antecedent.

Let's look at each guideline in detail.

1. A pronoun must clearly refer to a single antecedent. A common writing and speech problem occurs when the same pronoun refers to more than one antecedent. For instance, in the last example in the previous section, *them* can refer to *guilt, unkindness,* or *your friends.*

   Remember that a pronoun replaces a noun. To make sure that your writing and speech are clear, always use the noun first before you use the pronoun. Clarify the sentence by replacing the unclear pronouns with nouns. That way, all the remaining pronouns will clearly refer to a single antecedent.

   > Guilt and unkindness can be emotionally destructive to you and your friends. You must get rid of *them.*

   Here are two ways you could rewrite this sentence:

   > Guilt and unkindness can be emotionally destructive to you and your friends. You must get rid of *these issues.*

   > Guilt and unkindness can be emotionally destructive to you and your friends. You must get rid of *these destructive emotions.*

2. Place pronouns close to their antecedents. If too many phrases come between a pronoun and its antecedent, the sentence can be difficult to read and understand. This can happen even if the intervening material is logically related to the rest of the sentence. Consider the following sentence:

   > After meeting a few guests, the President entered the reception. At that point, Senator Chin and the other elected officials began to pose for pictures. Even so, *he* did not join them.

   In this sentence *he* is too far away from its antecedent, the President. One solution is to replace *he* with *the President.* The other solution is to rewrite the sentences to move the pronoun closer.

   > After meeting a few guests, the President entered the reception. At that point, Senator Chin and the other elected officials began to pose for pictures. Even so, the President did not join them.

   > After meeting a few guests, the President entered the reception. He did not join Senator Chin and the other elected officials, even though they began to pose for pictures.

Quick Tip

When you start a new paragraph, repeat the noun from the previous paragraph rather than using a pronoun in its place. Repeating the noun (usually a name) can help your reader more easily follow your logic.

---

3. Make a pronoun refer to a definite antecedent. Be sure all pronouns refer to only one antecedent. The pronouns *it, this, that,* and *which* are especially prone to unclear pronoun reference. Consider the following sentence:

   > I told my friends that I was going to be a rock star, which annoyed my mother.

   The following form is better because it is less ambiguous:

   > My mother was annoyed because I told my friends that I was going to be a rock star.

The Generic Masculine Pronoun

Pronouns have number, person, and gender.

Definition	Example
Number shows amount. (singular or plural)	Lenny has changed *his* plans. Lenny and Sam have changed *their* plans.
Person indicates whether the pronoun refers to the first person (*I:* the person speaking), second person (*you:* the person spoken to), or third person (*she:* person, place, or thing spoken about).	*I* like to read mysteries. *You* can get them in the library. *Jill* is studying math, which *she* needs.
Gender may be masculine, feminine, or neuter.	*He* is a butcher; *she* is a baker. *It* is a fine car.

Traditionally, a masculine pronoun was used to refer to a single antecedent whose gender is not specified.

> A student should turn in *his* assignments on time.

This usage is no longer considered correct, since it is sexist language. You can use both the masculine and feminine pronouns or recast the sentence to make the pronoun plural:

> A student should turn in *his or her* assignments on time.

> Students should turn in *their* assignments on time.

Which choice is best? Consider rewriting these sentences to make the pronoun plural because this results in smoother sentences.

Using *Who, Which, That*

Special rules govern the use of the relative pronouns *who, which,* and *that.*

1. *Who* refers to people or animals (only animals with names or special talents, like Lassie). She is not the actress *who* was originally cast in the role.
2. *That* and *which* refer to things, groups, and unnamed animals.

The choice between *which* and *that* depends on whether the clause introduced by the pronoun is *restrictive* or *nonrestrictive.*

- A *restrictive* clause is essential to the sentence.
- A *nonrestrictive* clause adds extra meaning, is set off by commas, and can be removed from the sentence.

Use *that* for restrictive clauses and *which* with nonrestrictive clauses.

> Once, at a social gathering, Gladstone said to Disraeli, "I predict, sir, *that* you will die either by hanging or by some vile disease." (restrictive clause)

> Disraeli replied, "*That* all depends, sir, upon whether I embrace your principles or your mistress." (restrictive clause)

> Postage meters, *which* are easy to use, are available at the book store. (nonrestrictive clause)

Quick Tip

In spoken English, *who* and *whomever* are becoming more and more uncommon. Informally, people use *who* and *whoever* in almost all situations.

It's a Wrap

✔ *Case* is the form of a noun or pronoun that shows how it is used in a sentence.

✔ English has three cases: *nominative, objective,* and *possessive.*

✔ Use the *nominative* case to show the subject of a verb; use the *objective* case to show the object of a verb; use the *possessive* case to show ownership.

✔ Make a pronoun clearly refer to a single, definite antecedent.

✔ Place pronouns close to their antecedents.

Test Yourself

QUESTIONS

True-False Questions

1. *Case* refers to the way a noun or pronoun changes, depending on how it is used in a sentence.

2. English has three cases: nominative, objective, and possessive.

3. In the *nominative case,* the pronoun is used to show possession.

4. In the *possessive case,* the pronoun is used as an object.

5. *Who* is in the nominative case; *whom* is in the objective case.

6. A *predicate nominative* is a noun or pronoun that follows a linking verb and identifies or renames the subject.

7. Use the objective case to show the object of a noun, verb, or adjective.

8. Gerunds always end in *-ed,* and they always function as verbs.

9. A pronoun used in apposition with a noun is in the same case as the noun.

10. A pronoun used as the subject of an infinitive is in the subjective case.

11. Pronouns that express ownership always take an apostrophe.

12. Use reflexive pronouns in place of subjects and objects.

13. A pronoun must clearly refer to a single, definite antecedent.

14. Place pronouns close to their antecedents.

15. *Who* refers to people or animals, while *that* and *which* refer to things, groups, and unnamed animals.

Completion Questions
Select the word that best completes each sentence.

1. Trish and (I, me) have decided to move to Brazil.

2. The new employees are (they, them).

3. The problem is unquestionably (she, her).

4. Human beings, (who, whom) are the most fascinating species on earth, are also the most admirable.

5. Those (whom, who) are early to bed and early to rise are healthy, wealthy, and very tired.

6. The best dressed employee has always been (him, he).

7. The winning contestants are the Griffels and (they, them).

8. The concept (which, that) intrigued (we, us) had not yet been publicized.

9. My car, (who, which) was brand new, had relatively little damage.

10. The car (which, that) hit me was speeding.

11. From (who, whom) did you buy that beautiful purse?

12. The thunderstorm frightened my cat and (I, me).

13. Please sit next to Rita and (me, I).

14. Brenda gave (he, him) a lot of unsolicited advice.

15. With (who, whom) have you agreed to carpool?

Multiple-Choice Questions
Select the best revision for each sentence.

1. When Harry and Chuck return home, he will call.
    (a) When Harry and Chuck return home, they will call.
    (b) When Harry and Chuck return home, Harry will call.

    (c) When Harry and Chuck return home, him will call.

    (d) When Harry and Chuck return home, calling will take place.

2. When Marcia spoke to Margery that morning, she did not realize that she would win the international bodybuilding contest.

    (a) When Marcia spoke to Margery that morning, her did not realize that she would win the international bodybuilding contest.

    (b) When Marcia spoke to Margery that morning, they did not realize that she would win the international bodybuilding contest.

    (c) When Marcia spoke to Margery that morning, Marcia did not realize that she would win the international bodybuilding contest.

    (d) When Marcia spoke to Margery that morning, no one realized that she would win the international bodybuilding contest.

3. When the rain started, we pulled out an umbrella. It annoyed the people around us, but we decided to stay at the ball field.

    (a) When the rain started, we pulled out an umbrella. It's annoyed the people around us, but we decided to stay at the ball field.

    (b) When the rain started, we pulled out an umbrella. Its annoyed the people around us, but we decided to stay at the ball field.

    (c) When the rain started, we pulled out an umbrella. The umbrella annoyed people around us, but we decided to stay at the ball field.

    (d) When the rain started, we pulled out an umbrella. They annoyed the people around us, but we decided to stay at the ball field.

4. If you asked Dick to describe Rudy, he would say that he was sly, boring, and cheap—and then he would snicker.

    (a) If you asked Dick to describe Rudy, Dick would say that he was sly, boring, and cheap—and then Dick would snicker.

    (b) If you asked Dick to describe Rudy, Dick would say that he was sly, boring, and cheap—and then he would snicker.

    (c) If you asked Dick to describe Rudy, he would say that he was sly, boring, and cheap—and then snickering would occur.

    (d) If you asked Dick to describe Rudy, Rudy would say that Rudy was sly, boring, and cheap—and then Dick would snicker.

5. They awarded we losers a gag prize.

    (a) They awarded them losers a gag prize.

    (b) They awarded yours losers a gag prize.

    (c) They awarded they losers a gag prize.

    (d) They awarded us losers a gag prize.

6. My neighbor agreed to support he for the condo board.

    (a) My neighbor agreed to support she for the condo board.

    (b) My neighbor agreed to support him for the condo board.

    (c) My neighbor agreed to support I for the condo board.

    (d) My neighbor agreed to support we for the condo board.

7. Naturally, you can invite whoever you want.

   (a) Naturally, you can invite who you want.

   (b) Naturally, you can invite which ever you want.

   (c) Naturally, you can invite whomever you want.

   (d) Naturally, you can invite that you want.

8. A student must understand that homework is very important to them.

   (a) Students must understand that homework is very important to them.

   (b) A student must understand that homework is very important to him.

   (c) A student must understand that homework is very important to her.

   (d) A student must understand that homework is very important to I.

9. The story was good, but they didn't explain what happened in the end.

   (a) The story was good, but he didn't explain what happened in the end.

   (b) The story was good, but the author didn't explain what happened in the end.

   (c) The story was good, but she didn't explain what happened in the end.

   (d) The story was good, but explaining what happened in the end didn't happen.

10. Justin saw the ad on the web page yesterday, but he can't seem to find it today.

   (a) Justin saw the ad in the web page yesterday, but he can't seem to find the today.

   (b) Justin saw the ad in the web page yesterday, but he can't seem to find its today.

   (c) Justin saw the ad in the web page yesterday, but he can't seem to find today.

   (d) Justin saw the ad in the web page yesterday, but he can't seem to find the ad today.

ANSWER KEY

True-False Questions

1. T   2. T   3. F   4. T   5. T   6. F   7. F   8. T   9. F   10. F   11. F   12. F
13. T   14. T   15. T

Completion Questions

1. I   2. they   3. she   4. who   5. who   6. he   7. they   8. that, us   9. which
10. that   11. whom   12. me   13. me   14. him   15. whom

Multiple-Choice Questions

1. b   2. c   3. c   4. a   5. d   6. b   7. c   8. a   9. b   10. d

CHAPTER 3

Using Verbs Correctly

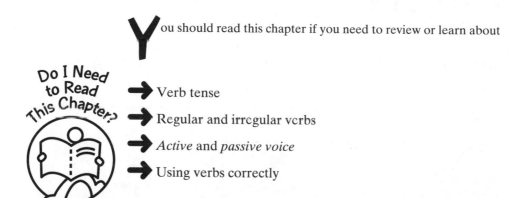

Y ou should read this chapter if you need to review or learn about

➡ Verb tense

➡ Regular and irregular verbs

➡ *Active* and *passive voice*

➡ Using verbs correctly

Get Started

In English, *tense* is used to show when something happens. Here, you will discover how verbs are formed and how they are used to show time. *Note:* This chapter is especially important for speakers of English as a second language.

Overview of Verb Functions

Recall from Chapter 1 that *verbs* are words that name an action or describe a state of being. There are four basic types of verbs: *action verbs, linking verbs, helping verbs,* and *verb phrases.* Verbs also convey information through changes in their form. Here are the five different things we find out from a verb:

- *Tense* (when the action takes place: past, present, or future)
- *Person* (who or what experiences the action)
- *Number* (how many subjects act or receive the action)
- *Mood* (the attitude expressed toward the action)
- *Voice* (whether the subject acts or is acted upon: the active or passive voice)

The Six Verb Tenses

The *tense* of a verb shows its time. English has six verb tenses. Each of the six tenses has two forms: *basic* and *progressive* (also known as "perfect"). The *basic* form shows action, occurrence, or state of being that is taking place right here and now. The basic form also is the base for the future form (i.e., *I will sleep; they will sleep*).

The following chart shows the six forms for the verb *to walk:*

Tense	Basic Form	Progressive Form
Present	walk	am walking
Past	walked	was walking
Future	will walk	will be walking
Present perfect	have walked	have been walking
Past perfect	had walked	had been walking
Future perfect	will have walked	will have been walking

The tense of English verbs is formed from helping verbs and principal parts. Each English verb has four main parts, as shown in the chart on the next page.

Principal Verb Parts

Present	Present Participle	Past	Past Participle
look	looking	looked	looked
dance	dancing	danced	danced

1. The present tense

   The *present* is used to form the present tense ("I look") and the future ("I will look"). English uses the helping verb *will* to show the future tense.

2. The present participle

   The *present participle* forms all six of the progressive forms ("I am looking," "I was looking," and so on).

3. The past tense

   The *past* forms only one tense, the past. As with the present tense, the principal part stands alone.

4. The past participle

   The *past participle* forms the last three tenses: the *present perfect* ("I have looked"), *the past perfect* ("I had looked"), and the *future perfect* ("I will have looked"). To form the past participle, start with a helping verb such as *is, are, was, has been.* Then add the principal part of the verb.

Quick Tip

When you *conjugate* a verb, you list the singular and plural forms of the verb in a specific tense.

Regular and Irregular Verbs

English verbs are divided into two classes: *regular* and *irregular*. These classifications come from the way the verb forms its past tense and past participles.

- *Regular verbs:* The past tense and past participle forms are created by adding *-d, -ed,* or *-t* to the present form, but the vowel doesn't change; for example, *walk, walked, walked.*

- *Irregular verbs:* No pattern is followed when the past and past participle are formed. Instead, there are many different forms. For example, with some irregular verbs the vowel changes and an *-n* or *-e* is added, as in *begin, began, begun.* With other verbs, the vowel changes and a *-d* or *-t* is added, as in *lose, lost, lost.*

Of all the verbs in English, *lie* and *lay* are likely the most often confused. *Lay* is a regular verb; *lie* is an irregular verb.

- *Lie* means "to repose." *Lie* conjugates as *lie, lay, lain.*
- *Lay* means "to put." *Lay* conjugates as *lay, laid, laid.*

Because *lay* is both the present tense of *to lay* and the past tense of *to lie,* many speakers and writers use *lay* when they mean *lie.*

- *Lie* is an intransitive verb. That means that it never takes a direct object.
  When people are exhausted, they should *lie* down for a rest.
- *Lay* is a transitive verb. That means that *lay* always takes a direct object.
  Lay the papers down.

The following chart lists some of the most common irregular verbs that have the same present participle, past, and past participle forms.

Present Tense	Present Participle	Past	Past Participle
bid	bidding	bid	have bid
burst	bursting	burst	have burst
cost	costing	cost	have cost
hit	hitting	hit	have hit
hurt	hurting	hurt	have hurt
kneel	knelt	knelt	have knelt
let	letting	let	have let
put	putting	put	have put
set	setting	set	have set

The next chart lists some of the most common irregular verbs that have the same past and past participle forms.

Present Tense	Present Participle	Past	Past Participle
beat	beat	beaten	have beaten
become	became	become	have become
bend	bent	bent	have bent
bind	binding	bound	have bound
bite	bit	bitten	have bitten

Present Tense	Present Participle	Past	Past Participle
bring	bringing	brought	have brought
build	building	built	have built
buy	buying	bought	have bought
catch	caught	caught	have caught
creep	crept	crept	have crept
dig	dug	dug	have dug
dive	dived or dove	dived	have dived
find	finding	found	have found
fight	fighting	fought	have fought
forget	forgot	forgotten	have forgotten
forgive	forgave	forgiven	have forgiven
get	getting	got	have gotten, have got
grow	grew	grown	have grown
hang	hung	hung	have hung
hang (execute)	hanged	hanged	have hanged
hide	hid	hidden	have hidden
hold	holding	held	have held
keep	keeping	kept	have kept
lay	laying	laid	have laid
lead	leading	led	have led
lose	losing	lost	have lost
pay	paying	paid	have paid
prove	proved	proved, proven	have proved, have proven
ring	rang	rung	have rung
say	saying	said	have said
send	sending	sent	have sent
show	showing	showed	have showed, have shown
sit	sitting	sat	have sat
sleep	sleeping	slept	have slept
spend	spending	spent	have spent
spin	spinning	spun	have spun
stand	standing	stood	have stood
stick	sticking	stuck	have stuck
teach	teaching	taught	have taught

Quick Tip

The most irregular verb in English is *to be.* Its principal parts are *be, being, was, were, been, am, are, is.*

The following chart lists some of the most common irregular verbs that change in unpredictable ways:

Present Tense	Present Participle	Past	Past Participle
arise	arising	arose	have arisen
begin	beginning	began	have begun
blow	blowing	blew	have blown
break	breaking	broke	have broken
choose	choosing	chose	have chosen
come	coming	came	have come
dive	dived, dove	dived	have dived
do	doing	did	have done
draw	drawing	drew	have drawn
drink	drinking	drank	have drunk
eat	eating	ate	have eaten
fall	falling	fell	have fallen
fly	flying	flew	have flown
freeze	freezing	froze	have frozen
give	giving	gave	have given
go	going	went	have gone
know	knowing	knew	have known
lie (horizontal)	lying	lay	have lain
ride	riding	rode	have ridden
rise	rising	rose	have risen
run	running	ran	have run
see	seeing	saw	have seen
shake	shaking	shook	have shaken
shrink	shrinking	shrank	have shrunk
sing	singing	sang	have sung
sink	sinking	sank	have sunk

Present Tense	Present Participle	Past	Past Participle
speak	speaking	spoke	have spoken
spring	springing	sprang	have sprung
steal	stealing	stole	have stolen
strive	striving	strove	have striven
swear	swearing	swore	have sworn
swim	swimming	swam	have swum
take	taking	took	have taken
tear	tearing	tore	have torn
throw	throwing	threw	have thrown
wake	waking	woke, waked	have woken, waked
wear	wearing	wore	have worn
write	writing	wrote	have written

How to Use Tenses

The six tenses express time within three main categories: *past*, *present*, and *future*. You want to use the tenses correctly so that you can show how one event is related to another. The following chart shows how the tenses are related.

Verb Tense and Time

Past	Present	Future
Simple past	Simple present	Simple future
Present perfect		Future perfect
Past perfect		
Past progressive	Present	Future progressive
Present perfect progressive		Future perfect progressive
Past perfect progressive		

- Use the two present forms (*simple present, present progressive*) to show events that take place now.
- Use the six past forms (*simple past, present perfect, past perfect, past progressive, present perfect progressive, past perfect progressive*) to show events that took place before the present.

- Use the four future forms (*simple future, future perfect, future progressive, future perfect progressive*) to show events that take place in the future.

1. Use past tenses accurately.

   The six past tenses all indicate the past in a different way. The following chart provides examples of how to use these tenses.

Tense	Use	Example
Simple past	Completed action (indefinite time)	We washed the car.
	Completed condition (indefinite time)	We were happy the party was over.
	Completed action (definite time)	We washed the car yesterday.
	Completed condition (definite time)	I was delighted yesterday to receive the news.
Present perfect	Completed action (indefinite time)	We have bought the gifts.
	Completed condition (indefinite time)	I have been very relieved.
	Action continuing into the present	Sarah has called for two hours.
	Condition continuing into the present	She has been in New York for a week.
Past perfect	Action completed before another	Greg had called all his friends before the party started.
	Condition completed	Greg had been a butcher before he became a guru.
Past progressive	Continuous completed action	I was attending a spa that month.
Present perfect progressive	Action continuing into present	Ralph has been exercising all week.
Past perfect progressive	Continuing action interrupted by another	Katie had been repairing the fence that was damaged in the storm.

2. Use future tenses accurately.

   The chart on the next page explains the future tenses.

Tense	Use	Example
Simple future	Future action	The bus will arrive.
	Future condition	I will be shocked when it does.
Future perfect	Future action completed before another	By the time you read this, the bus will have arrived.
	Future condition completed before another	The storm will have been raging for an hour before the phone goes out.
Future progressive	Continuing future action	Janice will be exercising all summer.
Future perfect progressive	Continuing future action completed before another	When we go on vacation next week, I will have been exercising for a month.

3. Don't switch tenses in midstream.

Never shift tenses in the middle of a sentence or a paragraph because it confuses readers. This guideline is especially important if your sentence contains more than one verb.

Incorrect: I *thought* I *had broken* the CD player when I *dropped* it on the floor, but it sud-
     past   past perfect   past

denly *begins* to play!
  present

Correct: I *thought* I *had broken* the CD player when I *dropped* it on the floor, but it sud-
    past   past perfect   past

denly *began* to play!
  past

Active and Passive Voice

In addition to showing time through tense, action verbs also show whether the subject performs the action or receives the action. This is called a verb's *voice*. English verbs have two voices: *active* and *passive*. (Linking verbs do not show voice.)

1. A verb is *active* when the subject performs the action.

We took the package home. ("We" are doing the action.)

I served a delicious meal. ("I" am doing the serving.)

Notice that in the active voice, the sentence starts with the subject. The first sentence starts with *We*. The second sentence starts with *I*.

2. A verb is *passive* when its action is performed upon the subject.

A package was taken home. (The speaker is not indicated.)

A delicious meal was served by me.

Notice that in the passive voice, the sentence *does not* start with the subject. The first sentence starts with the object, "a package." The second sentence starts with the object, "a delicious meal."

In general, use the active voice whenever possible because it is more direct and forceful. Using the active voice makes your writing crisp and powerful. The active verb is one word rather than two. Further, there is no need for a prepositional phrase beginning with "by" if you use the active voice.

Using the passive voice is preferable over the active voice under two conditions:

- You don't want to assign blame.
  A mistake occurred with the filing system.

Not surprisingly, the passive voice is very often found in business writing and speech. This helps the writer or speaker avoid "finger pointing."

- You don't know who did the action.
  A prank phone call was made at 2:00 A.M.

✔ A verb's *tense* shows when the action takes place. Use the right order of tenses to show the correct order of events.

✔ English verbs are divided into two classes: *regular* and *irregular.* These classifications come from the way the verb forms its past tense and past participles.

✔ *Voice* shows whether the subject acts (*active voice*) or is acted upon (*passive voice*). In general, use the *active voice* instead of the *passive voice.*

QUESTIONS

True-False Questions

1. English has six verb tenses. Each of the six tenses has two forms: basic and progressive (also known as "perfect").

2. The progressive form shows action, occurrence, or state of being that is taking place right here and now.

3. The tense of English verbs is formed from helping verbs and principal parts.

4. There are eight different past tenses. Each one indicates a subtle shift in time.

5. The past tense and past participle forms of irregular verbs are created by adding *-d, -ed,* or *-t* to the present form but the vowel doesn't change.

6. *Lie* means "to be in a reclining position." *Lie* conjugates to *lie, lay, lain.*

7. *Lay* means "to put down." *Lay* conjugates to *lay, laid, laid.*

8. Use the two past verb forms to show events that take place now.

9. Use the six past forms (simple past, present perfect, past perfect, past progressive, present perfect progressive, past perfect progressive) to show events that took place before the present.

10. Use the four future forms (*simple future, future perfect, future progressive, future perfect progressive*) to show events that take place in the future.

Completion Questions

Select the word that best completes each sentence.

1. Croatia (is, was) the first country to recognize the United States in 1776.

2. Ross Perot (resign, resigned, resigning) from the General Motors board of directors because of its decision to purchase Hughes Aircraft Company.

3. John Wilkes Booth (shotted, shot, shooted) Lincoln in a theater and was found in a warehouse.

4. Theodore Roosevelt (won, winned, wonned) the Nobel Prize for his arbitration of treaty discussions at the end of the Russo-Japanese War.

5. The Dominican Republic was called Santo Domingo when it first (gained, gain) independence.

6. The national anthem of the Netherlands is the oldest national anthem in the world: The music (appeart, appeared) in 1572, the lyrics in 1590.

7. James Garfield could (wrote, write) Latin with one hand and Greek with the other—simultaneously.

8. Before Bill Clinton, no left-handed American president had ever (serve, served) two terms.

9. Only three Presidents (have graduated, graduate) from the military academies: Grant and Eisenhower from West Point, and Carter from Annapolis.

10. The U.S. Constitution stipulates that, to be eligible for the Presidency, a candidate must be a natural-born citizen, must (have lived, live) in the United States for a minimum of 14 years, and must be at least 35 years old.

11. Franklin D. Roosevelt was the first U.S. president to have a presidential aircraft, but he only (flewed, flew) on the airplane once, to travel to the Yalta conference during World War II.

12. Of all U.S. presidents, none (live, lived) to be older than John Adams, who died at the age of 91.

13. John Quincy Adams (taked, took) his last skinny-dip in the Potomac on his seventy-ninth birthday.

14. All U.S. presidents (have worn, weared, have weared) glasses, but some of these men didn't like to be seen wearing eyeglasses in public.

15. When Harry Truman left office in 1952, he (get, got) in his own car and (drived, drove) himself back to Missouri.

Multiple-Choice Questions

Select the best answer for each question.

1. There are four basic types of verbs:
    (a) Action verbs, linking verbs, helping verbs, verb phrases
    (b) Helping verbs, action verbs, gerunds, participles
    (c) Helping verbs, verb phrases, active verbs, passive verbs
    (d) Action verbs, normal verbs, regular verbs, irregular verbs

2. When applied to verbs, the word *tense* indicates
    (a) How many subjects act or receive the action
    (b) Who or what experiences the action
    (c) When the action takes place: past, present, or future
    (d) The attitude expressed toward the action

3. To show the future tense, English uses the helping verb
    (a) Has
    (b) Have
    (c) Are
    (d) Will

4. The *past participle* forms all the following tenses *except*
    (a) Future perfect
    (b) The past perfect
    (c) Present perfect
    (d) The active voice

5. The past tense of the verb *to give* is
    (a) Gived
    (b) Gave
    (c) Have given
    (d) Gaved

6. The present participle of *to lie* (to be in a horizontal position) is
    (a) Lying
    (b) Lay
    (c) Have lain
    (d) Lie

7. The past tense of the verb *to freeze* is
   - (a) Freezed
   - (b) Have froze
   - (c) Froze
   - (d) Frozed

8. The past participle of the verb *to write* is
   - (a) Writing
   - (b) Have written
   - (c) Wrote
   - (d) Writed

9. The verb *to be* includes all the following principal parts *except*
   - (a) Being, was
   - (b) Has, have
   - (c) Been, am
   - (d) Are, is

10. Which of the following sentences is in the active voice?
    - (a) Plans for an assisted-living center were revealed by the city council at yesterday's meeting.
    - (b) The package was opened by my cousin Louie.
    - (c) At noon, the gates to the stadium were finally opened.
    - (d) A snail can sleep for three years.

11. Which of the following sentences is in the passive voice?
    - (a) The electric chair was invented by a dentist.
    - (b) A dentist invented the electric chair.
    - (c) You share your birthday with at least nine million other people in the world.
    - (d) You are more likely to be killed by a champagne cork than by a poisonous spider.

12. You should use the active voice whenever possible for all the following reasons *except*
    - (a) It creates a sentence that is direct and to the point.
    - (b) It creates a shorter sentence and is thus easier to read.
    - (c) It emphasizes the receiver of the action rather than the doer of the action.
    - (d) It emphasizes the doer of the action rather than the receiver of the action.

ANSWER KEY

True-False

1. T   2. F   3. T   4. F   5. F   6. T   7. T   8. F   9. T   10. T

Completion Questions

1. was   2. resigned   3. shot   4. won   5. gained   6. appeared   7. write
8. served   9. have graduated   10. have lived   11. flew   12. lived   13. took
14. have worn   15. got, drove

Multiple-Choice Questions

1. a   2. c   3. d   4. d   5. b   6. a   7. c   8. b   9. b   10. d   11. a   12. c

PART 2

Usage and Abusage

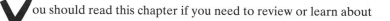

CHAPTER 4

Using Adjectives and Adverbs Correctly

Y ou should read this chapter if you need to review or learn about

Do I Need to Read This Chapter?

➡ Distinguishing between adjectives and adverbs

➡ Comparing with adjectives and adverbs

➡ Using adjectives and adverbs correctly

➡ Avoiding errors with adjectives and adverbs

Get Started

Recall from Chapter 1 that *adjectives* and *adverbs* are modifiers: They tell about a word by describing it. In this chapter, you will learn how to use adjectives and adverbs accurately as you describe people, places, things, and actions. This will make your writing and speech correct as well as colorful!

Is It an Adjective or an Adverb?

Both adjectives and adverbs describe other words.

- *Adjectives* describe a noun or pronoun.
- *Adverbs* describe a verb, adjective, or other adverb.

Quick Tip

Many adverbs are formed by adding *-ly* to an adjective (*poor* → *poorly*; *gentle* → *gently*), but a number of common adverbs do not follow this pattern.

Further, some words can be either adjectives or adverbs, depending on how they are used in a sentence.

Adjective: It was a *hard exam.*
                 adj. noun
Adverb: I *studied hard* all week.
          verb adv.
Adjective: Herman took the *late plane* back to Washington.
                  adj. noun
Adverb: Many of the guests *stayed late,* so we turned off the lights and went to bed.
              verb adv.

Therefore, the only reliable way to tell the difference between adjectives and adverbs is to analyze their function in a sentence. The following chart shows you how to examine sentences to distinguish between adjectives and adverbs.

Modifier	Function	Example
Adjective	Describe nouns	I went to an *early class.* adj. noun
Adjective	Describe pronouns	*They* were *suffering* with the flu for days. pronoun adj.
Adverb	Describe verbs	Mia *awoke early* in the morning. verb adv.
Adverb	Describe adverbs	Mia awoke *very early* in the morning. adv. adv.
Adverb	Describe adjectives	The dawn was *really beautiful.* adv. adj.

Positive, Comparative, and Superlative Degrees of Comparison

Adjectives and adverbs not only describe things; they also compare them. Adjectives and adverbs have different forms to show degrees of comparison. There are three degrees of comparison: *positive, comparative,* and *superlative.* The following list summarizes the three degrees of comparison:

- *Positive:* The base form of the adjective or adverb *not* being used in a comparison.
- *Comparative:* The form of the adjective or adverb being used to compare *two* things.
- *Superlative:* The form of the adjective or adverb being used to compare *three or more* things.

Here's a cheat sheet:

Degree of Comparison	Number of Things Compared	Example
Positive degree	None	Donald is *rich.*
Comparative degree	Two	Ross is *richer* than Donald.
Superlative degree	Three or more	Bill is the *richest* of all.

The following guidelines show how to form the comparative and superlative degrees of adjectives and adverbs.

1. In most cases, use *-er/-est* with one- and two-syllable adjectives or adverbs.

Positive	Comparative	Superlative
poor	poorer	poorest
rich	richer	richest
low	lower	lowest
high	higher	highest
large	larger	largest

2. When an adjective or adverb has three or more syllables, use *more* and *most* or *less* and *least* to form the comparative and superlative degrees.

Positive	Comparative	Superlative
uncommon	more uncommon	most uncommon
unusual	more unusual	most unusual
adorable	more adorable	most adorable
delightful	more delightful	most delightful
attractive	less attractive	least attractive
popular	less popular	least popular

3. If the word sounds awkward, break the rule.

   For example, since *just* has one syllable, the comparative form should be *juster* and the superlative form should be *justest*. However, since this sounds odd, we use *more just* and *most just*. Listen to the word to identify the most natural-sounding form of the comparative or superlative degree. When in doubt, consult your dictionary.

4. Never use both *-er* and *more,* or *-est* and *most,* with the same modifier.

   Never use double comparisons. For example, never say "the *most* furth*est*." Instead, say "furthest." Never say the "*least* happ*iest*." Instead, say "least happy."

5. All adverbs that end in *-ly* form their comparative and superlative degrees with *more* and *most*.

Positive	Comparative	Superlative
smoothly	more smoothly	most smoothly
easily	more easily	most easily
calmly	more calmly	most calmly
gracefully	more gracefully	most gracefully
gently	more gently	most gently

6. Some adjectives and adverbs have irregular forms.

   A few adjectives and adverbs don't follow these rules when they form the comparative and superlative degrees. Unfortunately, they are among the most commonly used modifiers in English, so you're apt to need them virtually every day. Since they don't follow a pattern, you just have to bite the bullet and memorize them.

Irregular Adjectives and Adverbs

Positive	Comparative	Superlative
bad	worse	worst
badly	worse	worst
far (distance)	farther	farthest
far	further	furthest
good	better	best
ill	worse	worst
late	later	later or latest
little (amount)	less	least
many	more	most
much	more	most
some	more	most
well	better	best

Good and *well* are especially tricky. Follow these guidelines:

- *Good* is always an adjective.
  You should read this novel: It has a *good plot*.
  adj. noun

  Rory traded in her old car for a *good one*.
  adj. noun

- *Well* is an adjective used to describe good health.
  You *look well* in that gorilla suit.
  verb adj.

  You *sound well*—for someone who has laryngitis.
  verb adj.

- *Well* is an adverb when used to describe anything but health.
  Chef Big Hat *cooks well*.
  verb adv.

  As a result, everyone in his house no doubt *eats well!*
  verb adv.

Comparing with Adjectives and Adverbs

Now that you know how to form the comparative and superlative forms of adjectives and adverbs, follow these guidelines to make the comparisons correct.

1. Use the comparative degree (*-er* or *more* form) to compare two things.
   - Your house is *bigger* than mine.
   - Your house has *more* rooms than mine.
2. Use the superlative form (*-est* or *most* to compare three or more things.
   - The kitchen is the *largest* room in the house.
   - It is the *most* impressive room of all.

Quick Tip

Fewer and *less* have different meanings and cannot be used interchangeably. *Fewer* refers to items that *can* be counted (*fewer sandwiches, fewer cookies*). *Less* refers to amounts that *can't* be counted (*less sugar, less sand, less anger, less filling*).

3. Use *other* and *else* correctly in comparisons.
   When you compare one item in a group with the rest of the group, be sure to include the word *other* or *else*. Then your comparison will make sense.
   Confusing comparison: Truman was greater than any American president.
   Logical comparison: Truman was greater than any *other* American president.
   Confusing comparison: The sinkhole in our front yard is deeper than any in the neighborhood.
   Logical comparison: The sinkhole in our front yard is deeper than any *other* in the neighborhood.
   Confusing comparison: Tina scored more points than anyone on the badminton team.
   Logical comparison: Tina scored more points than anyone *else* on the badminton team.
   Confusing comparison: The sumo wrestler is heavier than anyone in the competition.
   Logical comparison: The sumo wrestler is heavier than anyone *else* in the competition.
4. Create complete comparisons.
   Sentences that finish a comparison make sense. Comparisons that are incomplete or that compare illogical items become muddled. This confuses readers and obscures your point.
   Confusing comparison: Jack spends more time playing video games than homework.
   Logical comparison: Jack spends more time playing video games than *doing* homework.
   Confusing comparison: My suit is more stylish than Nick.
   Logical comparison: My suit is more stylish than *Nick's suit.*

Using Predicate Adjectives after Linking Verbs

A *predicate adjective* is an adjective that follows a linking verb and describes the subject of a sentence. Remember that *linking verbs* describe a state of being or a condition. They include all forms of *to be* (such as *am, is, are, were, was*) and verbs related to the senses (*look, smell, sound, feel*). Linking verbs connect the subject of a sentence to a word that renames or describes it.

Incorrect: This *goulash tastes deliciously.*
     noun link. adv.
        verb

Correct: This *goulash tastes delicious.*
     noun link. adj.
        verb

Use an adjective rather than an adverb after a linking verb. Therefore, use *delicious* rather than *deliciously* after the linking verb *tastes.*

Incorrect: The *child felt badly.*
      noun link. adv.
         verb

Correct: The *child felt bad.*
     noun link. adj.
        verb

Use an adjective rather than an adverb after a linking verb. Therefore, use *bad* rather than *badly* after the linking verb *felt.*

Incorrect: *I* *look awfully* in that shade of orange.
    pronoun link. adv.
        verb

Correct: *I* *look awful* in that shade of orange.
    pronoun link. adj.
        verb

Use an adjective rather than an adverb after a linking verb. Therefore, use *awful* rather than *awfully* after the linking verb *look.*

Incorrect *Sammi* *is* *happily.*
    noun link. adv.
       verb

Correct: *Sammi* *is* *happy.*
    noun link. adj.
       verb

Since *is* (a form of *to be*) is a linking verb, you must use the adjective *happy*, not the adverb *happily.*

Quick Tip

Some verbs do double duty: Sometimes they function as linking verbs, but other times they function as action verbs. As linking verbs, these verbs use adjectives as complements. As action verbs, these verbs use adverbs as complements.

Double Negatives

The following words are negatives:

Negative Words		
never	no	nobody
none	not	nothing
nowhere	n't	hardly
barely	scarcely	

Quick Tip

The most common negative words in English begin with *n.* Use this trick to help you remember these words.

Using two negative words in the same clause (group of words) creates a *double negative.* A *double negative* is an incorrect usage and should be avoided. To avoid this grammatical error, use only one negative word to express a negative idea.

Double negative: The traveler did *not* have *no* energy after the long flight.

Correct: The traveler did *not* have *any* energy after the long flight.

or

The traveler had *no* energy left after the long flight.

Double negative: Shakira could *not hardly* see in the blizzard.

Correct: Shakira could *hardly* see in the blizzard.

or

Shakira could *barely* see in the blizzard.

Double negatives are especially likely to cause problems when contractions are used. When the word *not* is used in a contraction—such as *isn't, doesn't, wouldn't, couldn't, don't*—the negative tends to slip by. As a result, writers and speakers may add another negative.

Double negative: Billy *didn't* bring *nothing* with him on vacation.

Correct: Billy *didn't* bring *anything* with him on vacation.

or

Billy brought *hardly* anything with him on vacation.

However, to create understatement, you can use a word with a negative prefix and another negative word. The two most common negative prefixes are *un-* and *-in.*

Nowadays, it is *not uncommon* to take six years to complete a four-year college degree. The report is *not inaccurate*, but no one should stake their reputation on it.

✔ Use an *adjective* to describe a noun or pronoun; use an *adverb* to describe a verb, adjective, or another adverb.

✔ Use the *comparative* degree to describe two items; use the *superlative* degree to describe three or more things.

✔ Be careful when you use an adjective after a linking verb.

✔ Avoid double negatives.

QUESTIONS

True-False Questions

1. Many adjectives are formed by adding *-ly* to an adverb.

2. Some words can be either adjectives or adverbs, depending on how they are used in a sentence.

3. The only reliable way to tell the difference between an adjective and an adverb is to memorize a list of words.

4. Adjectives and adverbs not only describe things, they also compare them.

5. The base form of the adjective or adverb not being used in a comparison is called the "positive degree."

6. The form of an adjective or adverb being used to compare two things is the "superlative degree."

7. The form of the adjective or adverb being used to compare three or more things is the "comparative degree."

8. To show comparison in most cases, use *-er/-est* with one- and two-syllable adjectives or adverbs.

9. When an adjective or adverb has three or more syllables, use *more* and *most* or *less* and *least* to form the comparative and superlative degrees.

10. Under certain conditions, you can use both *-er* and *more* or *-est* and *most* with the same modifier.

11. All adverbs that end in *-ly* form their comparative and superlative degrees with *more* and *most*.

12. The phrase "most smoothly" is in the superlative degree.

13. All adjectives and adverbs have irregular forms.

14. The superlative form of *bad* is *baddest*.

15. The superlative form of *far* is *furthest*.

16. *Good* is always an adjective.

17. *Well* is an adverb used to describe good health.

18. *Well* is an adjective used to describe anything but health.

19. Use the comparative degree (*-er* or *more*) to compare two things.

20. Use the superlative form (*-est* or *most*) to compare three or more things.

21. *Fewer* refers to items that *can't* be counted.

22. *Less* refers to amounts that *can* be counted.

23. When you compare one item in a group with the rest of the group, be sure to include the word *other* or *else*.

24. A *predicate adjective* is an adjective that follows a linking verb and describes the subject of a sentence.

25. Use an adverb rather than an adjective after a linking verb.

26. Using two negative words in the same clause (group of words) creates a *double negative*, which should be avoided.

27. *Hardly* is not a negative word.

28. To create overstatement, you can use a word with a negative prefix and another negative word.

Completion Questions

Select the word that best completes each sentence.

1. The elevator in my sister's apartment moves so (slowly, slow) we can make whoopee, conceive a child, and give birth before reaching her floor. And her apartment is on the first floor.

2. China has (most, more) English speakers than the United States.

3. The (longer, longest) town name in the world has 167 letters.

4. I've learned that you shouldn't compare yourself to the (better, best) others can do.

5. I've learned that two people can look at the exact same thing and see something (total, totally) different.

6. Every day (most, more) money is printed for Monopoly than for the U.S. Treasury.

7. My friend Fred is not the (brightest, brighter) light on the Ferris wheel.

8. If everything seems to be going (good, well), you have obviously overlooked something.

9. The grass is always (more greener, greener) when you leave the sprinkler on.

10. The (longer, longest) recorded flight of a chicken is 13 seconds.

11. The average person is about a quarter of an inch (tall, taller, tallest) in the morning.

12. The Neanderthal's brain was (big, bigger, biggest) than yours is.

13. Your right lung takes in (more, most) air than your left lung does.

14. Women's hearts beat (fast, faster, fastest) than men's hearts.

15. There are (more, most) plastic flamingos in America than real ones.

16. Each day is 0.00000002 seconds (long, longer, longest) than the one before because the Earth is gradually slowing down.

17. The total weight of all insects on Earth is 12 times (more great, greater, greatest, most greatest) than the weight of all the people on Earth.

18. There are more than three million lakes in Alaska. The (large, larger, largest), Lake Iliamna, is the size of Connecticut.

19. When North America was first settled, beavers there grew (bigger, biggest) than bears.

20. The (bright, brighter, brightest) star in the sky, Sirius, gives out 26 times as much light as the Sun.

21. The (older, oldest) national flag still in existence, that of Denmark, dates back to the thirteenth century.

22. The ashes of the metal magnesium are (more heavier, heavier) than magnesium itself.

23. Murphy's Oil Soap is the chemical (more, most) commonly used to clean elephants.

24. If things get any (worse, worst), I'll have to ask you to stop helping me.

25. How much (deep, deeper, deepest) would the ocean be if sponges didn't grow in it?

26. Nothing in the known universe travels (more fast, more faster, faster) than a bad check.

27. Did you hear about my new boyfriend? He's not the (sharper, sharpest) tool in the shed.

28. Good advice: Love (deep, deeply) and (most passionate, passionately). You might get hurt, but it's the only way to live life completely.

29. Talk (slow, slowly) but think (quick, quickly).

30. Doctor: "You're coughing (easier, easiest) today."
    Patient: "No wonder. I practiced all night."

Multiple-Choice Questions

Choose the best answer to each question.

1. *Adjectives* are modifiers that describe a
   (a) Noun or verb
   (b) Pronoun or adverb
   (c) Noun or pronoun
   (d) Verb or preposition

2. *Adverbs* are modifiers that describe all the following words except
   (a) Verbs
   (b) Pronouns
   (c) Adjectives
   (d) Adverbs

3. Which is the best revision of the following sentence? Nick's feet are bigger than Charles'.
   (a) Nick's feet are bigger than Charles' feet.
   (b) Nick's feet are more bigger than Charles" ' feet.
   (c) Nick's feet are biggest than Charles' feet.
   (d) Nick's feet are big than Charles'.

4. Each of the following is a degree of comparison *except*
   (a) Positive
   (b) Comparative
   (c) Superlative
   (d) Negative

5. What is the comparative form of *popular?*
   (a) Popularest
   (b) Popular
   (c) Most popular
   (d) More popular

6. The comparative and superlatives forms of *ill* are
   (a) Worse, most worse
   (b) Worster, worstest
   (c) worse, worst
   (d) More ill, most ill

7. The comparative and superlatives forms of *many* and *much* are
   (a) Double comparisons
   (b) Many, more
   (c) Regular
   (d) Identical

8. Which is the best revision of the following sentence?
   My brother's CD collection is larger than my son's.
   (a) My brother's CD collection is larger than my son's CD collection.
   (b) My brother's CD collection is large than my son's CD.
   (c) My brother's CD collection is largest than my son's CD.
   (d) My brother's CD collection is more larger than my son's CD collection.

9. Which is the best revision of the following sentence?
   In my opinion, collard greens is most delicious than broccoli.
   (a) In my opinion, collard greens is delicious than broccoli.
   (b) In my opinion, collard greens is deliciouser than broccoli.
   (c) In my opinion, collard greens is more delicious than broccoli.
   (d) In my opinion, collard greens is deliciously than broccoli.

10. All the following are negative words *except*
   (a) Scarcely
   (b) Hardly
   (c) Did
   (d) n't

11. Which is the best revision of the following sentence?
   Which of the twins writes gooder?
   (a) Which of the twins writes best?
   (b) Which of the twins writes better?
   (c) Which of the twins writes good?
   (d) Which of the twins writes more better?

12. Which of the following words best completes the sentence?
   Mr. Big is _____ willing to cooperate than his attitude suggests.
   (a) Less
   (b) Least
   (c) Leastest
   (d) Lesser

13. Which is the best revision of the following sentence?
   Two can live most cheaply than one.
   (a) Two can live cheaply than one.
   (b) Two can live moster cheaply than one.

(c) Two can live more cheaply than one.

(d) Two can live mostest cheaply than one.

14. When you are comparing a member of a group with the rest of the group, make sure that your sentence contains the words

(a) Than or if

(b) Good or worse

(c) More or better

(d) Other or else

15. Which of the following sentences is *not* correct?

(a) Nico could not see in the gloomy night.

(b) Nico could not hardly see in the gloomy night.

(c) Nico could barely see in the gloomy night.

(d) Nico had difficult seeing clearly in the gloomy night.

ANSWERS

True-False Questions

1. F   2. T   3. F   4. T   5. T   6. F   7. F   8. T   9. T   10. F   11. T   12. T
13. F   14. F   15. T   16. T   17. F   18. F   19. T   20. T   21. F   22. F
23. T   24. T   25. F   26. T   27. F   28. F

Completion Questions

1. slowly   2. more   3. longest   4. best   5. totally   6. more   7. brightest
8. well   9. greener   10. longest   11. taller   12. bigger   13. more   14. faster
15. more   16. longer   17. greater   18. largest   19. bigger   20. brightest
21. oldest   22. heavier   23. most   24. worse   25. deeper   26. faster
27. sharpest   28. deeply, passionately   29. slowly, quickly   30. easier

Multiple-Choice Questions

1. c   2. b   3. a   4. d   5. d   6. c   7. d   8. a   9. c   10. c   11. b   12. a
13. c   14. d   15. b

CHAPTER 5

Agreement: Matching Sentence Parts

Y ou should read this chapter if you need to review or learn about

➔ The grammatical subject of "agreement"

➔ Making subjects and verbs agree

➔ Making pronouns and antecedents agree

➔ Crafting smooth, logical sentences

Get Started

Agreement means that sentence parts match. Subjects must agree with verbs, and pronouns must agree with antecedents. If they don't, your sentences will sound awkward and may confuse your listeners and readers.

Like Peas in a Pod

Romeo and Juliet

Spaghetti and meatballs

Peanut butter and jelly

The birds and the bees

Some things just seem to go together well. We carry this concept over into grammar by matching all sentence parts. This matching of sentence elements is called *agreement*. It helps you create smooth and logical sentences.

The basic rule of sentence agreement is simple: *A subject must agree with its verb in number.* *Number* means singular or plural.

- A *singular* subject names *one* person, place, thing, or idea.
- A *plural* subject names *more than one* person, place, thing, or idea.

Here are some examples:

	Singular Subjects	**Plural Subjects**
Person:	I	they
Place:	beach	beaches
Thing:	desk	desks
Idea:	freedom	freedoms

1. Singular and plural nouns

    In English, the plurals of most nouns are formed by adding *-s* or *-es* to the singular form. For example: bike → bikes; race → races; inch → inches. Some nouns have irregular plurals, such as mouse → mice; woman → women, goose → geese. You can find the plural forms of irregular nouns in a dictionary.

2. Singular and plural pronouns

    Pronouns have singular and plural forms, too. Study the following chart.

Singular	**Plural**	**Singular or Plural**
I she, he it	we, they	you

3. Singular and plural verbs

As with nouns and pronouns, verbs show singular and plural forms. There are two areas in which you may have difficulty identifying singular and plural forms of nouns: the basic present tense and tenses using the helping verb *to be*.

As you study the following chart, notice that the form of the verb changes only in the third-person singular column, the middle column. Find the *-s* or *-es* added to the verb. That's the tricky part:

- Singular <u>verbs</u> end in *-s* or *-es*.
- Plural <u>nouns</u> end in *-s* or *-es*.

Here are some examples:

First and Second Person	Singular Third Person	Plural First, Second, Third Person
(I, you) begin	(he, she, it) begins	(we, you, they) begin
(I, you) do	(he, she, it) does	(we, you, they) do

As you can see from this chart, subject-verb agreement is most difficult to determine in the present tense.

4. Singular and plural forms of *be*

The form of the helping verb *be* may also help you determine whether a verb is singular or plural. The following chart shows the forms of *be* that are different from singular to plural.

Be Used as a Helping Verb

Singular	Plural
am	(we) are
(he, she, it) is	(they) are
(I, he, she, it) was	(we, they) were
(he, she, it) has been	(they) have been

A Singular Subject Must Have a Singular Verb

Now that you can recognize singular and plural nouns, pronouns, and verbs, you will be able to make all sentence parts agree in number. Remember the rule introduced in the beginning of this chapter: *A subject must agree with its verb in number.*

All the other rules follow from this one. The easiest rules are these two:

- A singular subject must have a singular verb.
- A plural subject must have a plural verb.

Let's examine the first rule.

5. A singular subject must have a singular verb.

    She   *hesitates* at all intersections, making the other drivers angry.
    sing. subject   sing. verb

    The singular subject *she* agrees with the singular verb *hesitates*.
    Procrastination is the art of keeping up with yesterday.
    sing. subject   sing. verb

    The singular subject *procrastination* agrees with the singular verb *is*.
    I   *am* ready for dinner now.
    sing. subject   sing. verb

    The singular subject *I* requires the singular verb *am*.

6. Two or more singular subjects joined by *or* or *nor* must have a singular verb.

    This makes perfect sense: You are making a choice between two singular subjects. The *or* shows that you are only choosing one.

    Either the dog   *or* the cat   *has* to go.
           sing. subject. or   sing. subject   sing. verb

    Only one pet will go—the dog or the cat. Therefore, you will only have one pet left. Two singular subjects—*dog* and *cat*—joined by *or* take the singular verb *has*.
    Neither Elvis Costello *nor* Elvis Presley *is* in the room.
          sing. subject   nor sing. subject   sing. verb

    Each subject is being treated individually. Therefore, two singular subjects—*Elvis Costello* and *Elvis Presley*—joined by *nor* take the singular verb *is*.

7. Subjects that are singular in meaning but plural in form require a singular verb.

    These subjects include words such as *measles, civics, social studies, mumps, molasses, news, economics,* and *mathematics*.

    The *news*   *is* on very night at 11:00 P.M.
        sing. subject   sing. verb

    The singular subject *news* takes the singular verb *is*.

8. Plural subjects that function as a single unit take a singular verb.

    Spaghetti and meatballs is my favorite dish.
    sing. subject   sing. verb

    The singular subject *spaghetti and meatballs* requires the singular verb *is*.
    Bacon and eggs makes a great late night snack.
    sing. subject   sing. verb

    The singular subject *bacon and eggs* agrees with the singular verb *makes*.

9. Titles are always singular.
It doesn't matter how long the title is, what it names, or whether or not it sounds plural—a title always takes a singular verb.
For Whom the Bell Tolls is a story about the Spanish Civil War.
sing. subject   sing. verb

The singular title *For Whom the Bell Tolls* requires the singular verb *is*.
Stranger in a Strange Land was written by Robert Heinlein.
sing. subject   sing. verb

The singular title *Stranger in a Strange Land* requires the singular verb was.

Most measurements are singular—even though they look plural. For example: "*Half a dollar is* more than enough" (not "*are* more than enough").

A Plural Subject Must Have a Plural Verb

Just as a singular subject requires a singular verb, so a plural subject requires a plural verb. Here are some examples:

1. A plural subject must have a plural verb.
Men   are from Earth. *Women   are* from Earth. Deal with it.
plural   plural   plural   plural
subject verb   subject verb

The plural subject *men* requires the plural verb *are*. The plural subject *women* requires the plural verb *are*.

On average, *people   fear* spiders more than *they   do* death.
          plural   plural   plural   plural
          subject verb   subject verb

The plural subject *people* requires the plural verb *fear* (not the singular verb *fears*). The plural subject *they* requires the plural verb *do* (not the singular verb *does*).

Students at U.S. colleges *read* about 60,000 pages in four years.
plural   plural
subject   verb

The plural subject *students* requires the plural verb *read* (not the singular verb *reads*).
Facetious and *abstemious contain* all the vowels in the correct order, as does arsenious,
        plural   plural
        subject   verb
meaning "containing arsenic."

The plural subject *facetious and abstemious* requires the plural verb *contain* (not the singular verb *contains*.) Think of the conjunction *and* as a plus sign. Whether the parts of the subject joined by *and* are singular or plural (or both), they all add up to a plural subject and so require a plural verb.

2. Two or more plural subjects joined by *or* or *nor* must have a plural verb.

This is the logical extension of the rule you learned earlier about two or more singular subjects joined by *or* or *nor* taking a singular verb. Here, since both subjects are plural, the verb must be plural as well.

Either the *children or* the *adults*   *are* clearing the table.

     plural   plural   plural
     subject   subject   verb

Since both subjects are plural, one of them alone is still plural. Therefore, two plural subjects—*children* and *adults*—joined by *or* take the plural verb *are.*

Neither my *relatives nor* my *friends*   *are* leaving any time soon.

     plural   plural   plural
     subject   subject   verb

Since both subjects are plural, one of them alone is still plural. Therefore, two plural subjects—*relatives* and *friends*—joined by *nor* take the plural verb *are.*

3. A compound subject joined by *and* is plural and must have a plural verb.

The conjunction *and* acts like a plus (+) sign, showing that $1 + 1 = 2$ (or $1 + 1 + 1 = 3$, etc.).

Brownies and ice cream are a spectacular dessert.

sing.   sing.   plural
subject   subject   verb

Brownies and ice cream = two desserts. $1 + 1 = 2$. Therefore, the verb must be plural: are.

Nina and Christopher have donated money to charity.

sing.   sing.   plural
subject   subject   verb

Nina and Christopher = two people. $1 + 1 = 2$. Therefore, the verb must be plural: have.

4. If two or more singular and plural subjects are joined by *or* or *nor,* the subject closest to the verb determines agreement.

This is basically an exception made for the sake of sound: It sounds better to match the verb to the closer subject.

Margery or the *twins*   *are* coming on the trip to Seattle.

sing.   plural   plural
subject   subject   verb

Since the plural subject *twins* is closest to the verb, the verb is plural: *are.*

The *twins or Margery is* coming on the trip to Seattle.

    plural   sing.   sing.
    subject   subject   verb

Since the singular subject *Margery* is closest to the verb, the verb is singular: *is.*

Collective Nouns and Indefinite Pronouns

A *collective noun* names a group of people or things. Collective nouns include the words *class, committee, flock, herd, team, audience, assembly, team,* and *club.* Collective nouns can be singular or plural, depending on how they are used in a sentence. Here are the basic guidelines:

- A collective noun is considered *singular* when it functions as a single unit. Collective nouns used as one unit take a singular verb.
- A collective noun is considered *plural* when the group it identifies is considered to be individuals. Collective nouns that indicate many units take a plural verb.

Here are some examples:

The *team*   *has practiced* for tonight's big game for months.
   sing.   sing.
   subject   verb

The singular subject *team* agrees with the singular verb *has practiced* because in this instance, the team functions as one (singular) group.

The *team*   *have practiced* for tonight's big game for months.
   plural   plural
   subject   verb

The subject *team* becomes plural because each member of the group is now being considered as an individual.

Indefinite pronouns, like collective nouns, can be singular or plural, depending on how they are used in a sentence. Indefinite pronouns refer to people, places, objects, or things without pointing to a specific one. Indefinite pronouns include words such as *everyone, someone, all,* and *more.*

- Singular indefinite pronouns take a singular verb.
- Plural indefinite pronouns take a plural verb.

The following chart shows singular and plural indefinite pronouns. The chart also shows pronouns that can be either singular or plural, depending on how they are used in a sentence.

Singular	Plural	Singular or Plural
another	both	all
anybody	few	any
anyone	many	more
anything	others	most
each	several	none
either		some
everyone		
everybody		
everything		
little		
many a		

Continues

Singular	Plural	Singular or Plural
much		
neither		
nobody		
no one		
nothing		
one		
other		
somebody		
someone		
something		

Look back at the chart. You will see that the following patterns emerge:

1. Indefinite pronouns that end in -*body* are always singular. These words include *anybody, somebody, nobody*.

2. Indefinite pronouns that end in -*one* are always singular. These words include *anyone, everyone, someone,* and *one*.

3. The indefinite pronouns *both, few, many, others,* and *several* are always plural.

4. The indefinite pronouns *all, any, more, most, none,* and *some* can be singular or plural, depending on how they are used.

Here are some examples:

One of the gerbils *is* missing.
sing.   sing.
subject   verb

The singular subject *one* requires the singular verb *is*.

Both of the gerbils *are* missing.
plural   plural
subject   verb

The plural subject *both* requires the plural verb *are*.

All of the beef stew *was* devoured.
sing.   sing.
subject   verb

In this instance, *all* is being used to indicate one unit. As a result, it requires the singular verb *was*.

Many of the guests *are* sick of Tedious Ted's endless chatter.

plural   plural
subject   verb

The plural subject *many* requires the plural verb *are*.

Special Problems in Agreement

The rules for agreement are straightforward, but some thorny problems do arise. Here are the two most challenging issues: hard-to-find subjects and intervening phrases.

1. Identify hard-to-find subjects.

    Some subjects can be harder to find than others. Subjects that come before the verb are especially tricky. However, a subject must still agree in number with its verb, as the following examples show:

    In the bottom of the lake are two old cars.

              plural   plural
              verb   subject

    Quick Tip

    The words *there* or *here* at the beginning of a sentence often signal inverted word order.

    The plural subject *cars* agrees with the plural verb *are*.

    There *were* still half a dozen *tires* in the lake, too.

    plural   plural
    verb   subject

    The plural subject *tires* requires the plural verb *were*.

2. Ignore intervening phrases.

    Disregard words or phrases that come between the subject and the verb. A phrase or clause that comes between a subject and its verb does not affect subject-verb agreement.

    The strongest *muscle*   *in the body is* the tongue.

            sing.   prep.   sing.
            subject phrase   verb

The singular subject *muscle* agrees with the singular verb *is*. Ignore the intervening prepositional phrase "in the body."

The *captain*   *of the guards stands* at the door of Buckingham Palace.

    sing.   prep.   sing.
    subject phrase   verb

The singular subject *captain* agrees with the singular verb *stands*. Ignore the intervening prepositional phrase "of the guards."

Agreement of Pronouns and Antecedents

Like subjects and verbs, pronouns and antecedents (the words to which they refer) must agree. Follow these rules to make sure that your pronouns and antecedents match.

1. A pronoun agrees (or matches) with its antecedent in *number, person,* and *gender.*

    Hortense gave half her cupcake to Shirley.

    Both the antecedent *Hortense* and the pronoun *her* are singular in number, in the third person, and feminine in gender.

    Errors often occur when there are incorrect shifts in person and gender.

    Error: *Hortense* will eat her bran flakes and tofu, which *you* need to stay healthy.

    Correct: *Hortense* will eat her bran flakes and tofu, which *she* needs to stay healthy.

2. Use a singular personal pronoun with a singular indefinite pronoun.

    If *anyone* questions the edict, refer *him* or *her* to the boss.

    The singular pronouns *him* or *her* refer to the singular pronoun *anyone.*

3. Use a plural pronoun when the antecedents are joined by *and.* This is true even if the antecedents are singular.

    The *dog* and *cat* maintain *their* friendship by staying out of each other's way.

        sing.   sing.   plural
        subject subject   pronoun

    Since the two singular antecedents *dog* and *cat* are joined by *and,* use the plural pronoun *their.* This is a case of $1 + 1 = 2$ (one dog + one cat = two pets).

4. Antecedents joined by *or, nor,* or correlative conjunctions such as *either . . . or, neither . . . nor* agree with the antecedent closer to the pronoun.

    Neither my baby *sister* or the *twins* sleep in *their* bed.

             sing.   plural   plural
             subject subject   pronoun

    Use the plural pronoun *their* to agree with the plural antecedent *cats.*

    Neither the *twins* nor my baby *sister* sleeps in *her* bed.

          plural   sing.   sing.
          subject   subject   pronoun

    Use the singular pronoun *her* to agree with the singular antecedent *sister.*

5. Be sure that the pronoun refers directly to the noun.

    Confusion occurs when the pronoun can refer to more than one antecedent. If you end up with a confusing sentence, rewrite the sentence.

    Confusing: Norman saw a coupon in last year's newspaper, but he can't find *it.*

    What is it that Norman can't find: the coupon or the newspaper?

    Correct: Norman can't find the coupon he saw in last year's newspaper.

It's a Wrap

✔ *Agreement* means that sentence parts match.

✔ Subjects must agree with verbs, and pronouns must agree with antecedents.

✔ Find the sentence's subject. Figure out if the subject is singular or plural. Select the appropriate verb form to match the form of the subject.

Test Yourself

QUESTIONS

True-False Questions

1. A subject must agree with its verb in number. *Number* means singular or plural.

2. A *plural* subject names *one* person, place, thing, or idea.

3. A *singular* subject names *more than one* person, place, thing, or idea.

4. In English, the plural of most nouns is formed by adding *-s* or *-es* to the singular form.

5. Pronouns do not have singular and plural forms.

6. Verbs also show singular and plural forms.

7. The form of the verb changes only in the third-person singular form.

8. A plural subject must have a singular verb. A singular subject must have a plural verb.

9. Two or more singular subjects joined by *or* or *nor* must have a singular verb.

10. Subjects that are singular in meaning but plural in form require a singular verb.

11. Plural subjects that function as a single unit take a plural verb.

12. Titles are always singular.

13. Two or more plural subjects joined by *or* or *nor* must have a plural verb.

14. A compound subject joined by *and* is singular and must have a singular verb.

15. If two or more singular and plural subjects are joined by *or* or *nor,* always use a plural verb.

16. A *collective noun* names a group of people or things.

17. *Collective nouns* are always plural, no matter how they are used in a sentence.

18. *Indefinite pronouns* can be singular or plural, depending on how they are used in a sentence.

19. Indefinite pronouns include words such as *everyone, someone, all,* and *more.*

20. When you are determining agreement, disregard words or phrases that come between the subject and the verb.

21. A pronoun agrees (or matches) with its antecedent in *number* and *person,* but not *gender.*

22. Use a singular personal pronoun with a singular indefinite pronoun.

23. In general, use a plural pronoun when the antecedents are joined by *and*. This is not true if the antecedents are singular.

24. Antecedents joined by *or, nor,* or correlative conjunctions such as *either . . . or, neither . . . nor* agree with the antecedent closer to the pronoun.

25. Agreement makes sentences sound smooth and logical.

26. The noun *car* is singular, but *cars* is plural.

27. The noun *tomatoes* is singular, but *tomato* is plural.

28. The noun *women* is singular, but *woman* is plural.

29. The pronoun *I* is singular, but *we* is plural.

30. The verb *stands* is singular, but *stand* is plural.

31. The verb *are* is singular, but *is* is plural.

32. The verb *was eating* is singular, but *were eating* is plural.

33. The verb *were* is singular, but *was* is plural.

34. The verb *grows* is singular, but *grow* is plural.

35. The verb phrase *have been watching* is singular, but *has been watching* is plural.

Completion Questions
Select the word that best completes each sentence.

1. The pop you get when you crack your knuckles (are, is) actually a bubble of gas bursting.

2. Polar bears (is, are) left-handed.

3. The name of all the continents (ends, end) with the same letter that they start with.

4. No president of the United States (were, was) an only child.

5. Everyone (are, is) entitled to my opinion.

6. Here is some good advice: Don't sneeze when someone (is, are) cutting your hair.

7. If a man (are, is) wearing a striped suit, it's against the law to throw a knife at him in Natoma, Kansas.

8. In 1659, Massachusetts (mades, made) Christmas illegal.

9. Unless you have a doctor's note, it (are, is) illegal to buy ice cream after 6 P.M. in Newark, New Jersey.

10. It is a misdemeanor to show movies that (depicts, depict) acts of felonious crime in Montana.

11. I (drives, drive) way too fast to worry about cholesterol.

12. If Barbie (are, is) so popular, why do you have to (buys, buy) her friends?

13. Many people (quits, quit) looking for work when they find a job.

14. A Rolling Stone (play, plays) the guitar.

15. It's always darkest just before I (open, opens) my eyes.

16. The squeaking wheel (get, gets) annoying.

17. A journey of a thousand miles (begin, begins) with a blister.

18. Don't count your chickens—it (take, takes) too long.

19. Donald Duck comics (was, were) banned from Finland because he doesn't wear pants.

20. *Kemo Sabe* (mean, means) "soggy shrub" in Navajo.

21. All porcupines (floats, float) in water.

22. The only nation whose name (begins, begin) with an *A* but doesn't end in an *A* is Afghanistan.

23. Emus cannot (walks, walk) backwards.

24. Most Americans' car horns (beep, beeps) in the key of "F."

25. No word in the English language (rhymes, rhyme) with *month*.

Multiple-Choice Questions

Choose the best answer to each question.

1. The American slogan for Salem cigarettes, "Salem-Feeling Free," _____ translated into the Japanese market as "When smoking Salem, you will feel so refreshed that your mind _____ to be free and empty."
   - (a) Was, seems
   - (b) Was, seem
   - (c) Were, seem
   - (d) Were, seems

2. Frank Perdue's chicken slogan, "It takes a strong man to make a tender chicken," _____ translated into Spanish as "It _____ an aroused man to make a chicken affectionate."
   - (a) Were, takes
   - (b) Were, take
   - (c) Was, takes
   - (d) Was, take

3. I had a linguistics professor who said that it's man's ability to use language that _____ him the dominant species on the planet. That may be. But I think there's one other thing that _____ us from animals. We aren't afraid of vacuum cleaners. —Jeff Stilson
   - (a) Make, separate
   - (b) Make, separates
   - (c) Makes, separate
   - (d) Makes, separates

4. According to the national average: Once someone _____ an elevator button, 58 seconds will pass before they will _____ it again. In New York, it's 11 seconds.

    (a) Push, push

    (b) Push, pushes

    (c) Pushes, push

    (d) Pushes, pushes

5. If police arrest a mime, do they _____ him he _____ the right to remain silent?

    (a) Tell, have

    (b) Tell, has

    (c) Tells, has

    (d) Tells, have

6. I've learned that it _____ years to build up trust and only seconds to destroy _____.

    (a) Takes, them

    (b) Takes, it

    (c) Take, them

    (d) Take, it

7. I've learned that either you _____ your attitude or it _____ you.

    (a) Control, controls

    (b) Control, control

    (c) Controls, control

    (d) Controls, controls

8. I've learned that our background and circumstances may have influenced who we _____, but we are responsible for who we _____.

    (a) Is, become

    (b) Is, becomes

    (c) Are, becomes

    (d) Are, become

9. I've learned that credentials on the wall do not _____ you a decent human being.

    (a) Made

    (b) Makes

    (c) Make

    (d) Making

10. Up to 3,000 species of trees _____ been cataloged in one square mile of the Amazon jungle.

    (a) Is

    (b) Was

(c) Has

(d) Have

Further Exercises

1. Correct all errors in agreement in the following paragraph.

   Two people left a 15-mile-long trail of doughnuts after they tooks a donut truck from a parking lot and fled, police said Thursday. The truck were parked at a convenience store with its rear doors open and its engine running while a deliveryman carried doughnuts inside, said a Slidell police spokesman. Two suspects hopped in the truck and sped off to the nearby town of Lacombe, with doughnuts spilling out along the way, he said. They abandoned the truck when they was spotted by police responding to reports of a dangerous driver who were losing his doughnuts. A passenger were captured, but the driver, whose name were not released, ran away.

   Their motive for taking the truck filled with donuts were unclear.

   "I don't know if it were a need for transportation or if they just had the munchies," the police said.

2. Correct all errors in agreement in the following paragraph.

   A wife are complaining about her husband spending all his time at the local tavern, so one night he take her along with him.

   "What'll ya have?" he ask.

   "Oh, I don't know. The same as you, I suppose," she reply.

   So the husband order a couple of Jack Daniels and gulp his down in one go.

   His wife watch him, then take a sip from her glass and immediately spit it out. "Yuck, it tastes awful, worse than awful!" she splutter. "I don't know how you can drink this stuff!"

   "Well, there you goes," cry the husband. "And you thinks I'm out enjoying myself every night!"

ANSWERS

True-False Questions

1. T   2. F   3. F   4. T   5. F   6. T   7. T   8. F   9. T   10. T   11. F   12. T
13. T   14. F   15. F   16. T   17. F   18. T   19. T   20. T   21. F   22. T   23. F
24. T   25. T   26. T   27. F   28. T   29. T   30. T   31. F   32. T   33. F   34. T
35. F

Completion Questions

1. is   2. are   3. ends   4. was   5. is   6. is   7. is   8. made   9. is   10. depict
11. drive   12. is, buy   13. quit   14. plays   15. open   16. gets   17. begins
18. takes   19. were   20. means   21. float   22. begins   23. walk   24. beep
25. rhymes

Multiple-Choice Questions

1. a   2. c   3. d   4. c   5. b   6. b   7. a   8. d   9. c   10. d

Further Exercises

1. Two people left a 15-mile-long-trail of doughnuts after they took a donut truck from a parking lot and fled, police said Thursday. The truck was parked at a convenience store with its rear doors open and its engine running while a deliveryman carried doughnuts inside, said a Slidell police spokesman. Two suspects hopped in the truck and sped off to the nearby town of Lacombe, with doughnuts spilling out along the way, he said. They abandoned the truck when they were spotted by police responding to reports of a dangerous driver who was losing his doughnuts. A passenger was captured, but the driver, whose name was not released, ran away.

   Their motive for taking the truck filled with donuts was unclear.

   "I don't know if it was a need for transportation or if they just had the munchies," the police said.

2. A wife is complaining about her husband spending all his time at the local tavern, so one night he takes her along with him.

   "What'll ya have?" he asks.

   "Oh, I don't know. The same as you, I suppose," she replies.

   So the husband orders a couple of Jack Daniels and gulps his down in one go.

   His wife watches him, then takes a sip from her glass and immediately spits it out. "Yuck, it tastes awful, worse than awful!" she splutters. "I don't know how you can drink this stuff!"

   "Well, there you go," cries the husband. "And you think I'm out enjoying myself every night!"

CHAPTER 6

The 25 Most Common Usage Problems

Y ou should read this chapter if you need to review or learn about

Do I Need to Read This Chapter?

➡ The most common writing errors

➡ Finding errors in your own writing

➡ Correcting these errors

Get Started

More than ever before, good writing is essential for success. Simple, straightforward, and correct writing saves time, creates good faith, and prevents misunderstandings. In this chapter, we'll concentrate on the *correct* part of this equation so your writing will be "letter perfect."

Top Trouble Spots in Writing

When someone complains that a person "can't write," they are most often referring to errors that person makes in grammar and usage. Below are the top 25 writing hot spots.

The 25 Top Writing Errors

Grammar and Usage

1. Lack of clarity
2. Redundancy (unnecessary words)
3. Problems with subject-verb agreement
4. Lack of parallel structure
5. Wrong verb tense
6. Mixed metaphors
7. Dangling modifiers
8. Misplaced modifiers
9. Incorrect idioms
10. Biased language
11. Incorrect voice (active versus passive voice)

Sentences

12. Fragments (incomplete sentences)
13. Run-ons (two sentences run together)

Spelling

14. Missing letters
15. Extra letters
16. Transposed letters
17. Incorrect plurals
18. Errors in confusing word pairs (such as *weather/whether*)

Punctuation

19. Missing commas or extra commas
20. Missing or misused apostrophes
21. Misused exclamation marks
22. Misused semicolons

Capitalization

23. Proper nouns not capitalized
24. Errors in titles

Proofreading

25. Missing words

Now, we will review each of these problem places so that you can have writing that is letter perfect.

Most Common Grammar and Usage Errors

1. Lack of clarity

   Incorrect: Prehistoric people used many inorganic substances difficult to find at archaeological sites, which included clay and rock.

   Correct: Prehistoric people used many inorganic substances, including clay and rock, which are difficult to find at archaeological sites.

   Sentences can be confusing for many different reasons. In the previous example, too many phrases come between the pronoun and its antecedent. As a result, the pronoun reference gets confusing. This can happen even if the intervening material is logically related to the rest of the sentence, as is the case here.

   Sentence construction is so important that it's covered in four chapters: Chapters 7, 8, 9, and 13. If you're having trouble constructing logical and cohesive sentences, review all these chapters. Here's the quick and dirty lowdown:

   • One sentence = one complete thought. Don't cram too much into one sentence.
   • The more complex your ideas, the shorter and more simple your sentences should be.
   • Check that all parts of the sentence are logically related. Are they in the same tense, for example?
   • Reread your sentences to make sure all pronouns refer to their antecedents and are placed as close as possible to them.
   • Check that you have punctuated your sentences correctly.

2. Redundancy (unnecessary words)

   Incorrect: If you reread your work, you will find upon serious reconsideration that a great deal of repetition can be avoided by careful editing and revising and attentive reevaluation. Scrupulous editing can also help you make your writing less wordy.

   Correct: If you reread your work, you will find that a great deal of repetition can be avoided by careful editing.

   Long-winded writing may sound educated and impressive, but it actually turns off your audience because it wastes their time. Say what you need to say concisely. Since your writing will be more intelligible, it will communicate its message directly.

3. Problems with subject-verb agreement

    Incorrect: Verbs has to agree with their subjects.

    Correct: Verbs have to agree with their subjects.

Agreement means that sentence parts match, singular to singular and plural to plural. Since the subject *verbs* is plural, it takes a plural verb, *agree.*

This is confusing because we add -*s* or -*es* to make the third-person *singular* form of most *verbs* but add -*s* or -*es* to make the *plural* form of most *nouns.* For example, *he starts* is singular, but *six papers* is plural. Both end in *s.* Agreement is covered in detail in Chapter 5.

4. Lack of parallel structure

    Not parallel: To avoid getting hit by lightning, never seek protection under a tree, lying down on wet ground, or staying on a bike.

    Parallel: To avoid getting hit by lightning, never seek protection under a tree, lie down on wet ground, or stay on a bike.

Parallel structure means putting ideas of the same rank in the same grammatical structure. Your writing (and speech) should have parallel words, phrases, and clauses.

- *Parallel words* share the same part of speech (such as nouns, adjectives, or verbs) and tense (if the words are verbs).
- *Parallel phrases* create an underlying rhythm in your speech and writing.
- *Parallel clauses* also give your writing balance.

Parallel structure is covered in detail in Chapter 9.

5. Wrong verb tense

    Incorrect: President John Quincy Adams *owns* a pet alligator, which he kept in the East Room of the White House.

    Correct: President John Quincy Adams *owned* a pet alligator, which he kept in the East Room of the White House.

The *tense* of a verb shows its time. English has six verb tenses. Each of the six tenses has two forms: *basic* and *progressive* (also known as "perfect"). In the example here, the action takes place in the past, so the past tense must be used. Verb tense is the subject of Chapter 3.

6. Mixed metaphors

    Incorrect: Take the bull by the toe.

    Correct: Take the bull by the horns.

Metaphors are figures of speech that compare two unlike things to explain the less-familiar object. When used correctly, metaphors make your writing more descriptive and precise. In most instances, metaphors use words for more than their literal meaning. Here, for example, we're not literally talking about grabbing a bull by the horns; rather, we're figuratively talking about seizing an opportunity.

For a metaphor to be effective, it must compare images or objects that go together. Here, for instance, we would grab a bull's horns, not its toes. When two clashing images are combined in one comparison, we get a *mixed metaphor,* which confuses readers.

7. Dangling modifiers

    Incorrect: Flying over the countryside, cars and houses looked like toys.

    Correct: As we flew over the countryside, cars and houses looked like toys.

A *modifier* is a word or phrase that describe a subject, verb, or object. (To "modify" is to qualify the meaning.). The modifier is said to "dangle" when the word it modifies has been left out of the sentence. Dangling modifiers confuse your readers and obscure your meaning because the sentence doesn't make sense.

Correct a dangling modifier by adding the word or words that have been left out. Here, the subject *we* was added and *flying* was changed to *flew* so the sentence makes sense.

And while we're dangling, let's look at another mangled construction, *dangling participles*. A *participle* is a verb ending in *-ing*. It is *dangling* when the subject of the participle and the subject of the sentence don't agree. For example:

Incorrect: Rushing to finish the paper, Bob's printer broke.

The subject is Bob's printer, but the printer isn't doing the rushing.

Correct: While Bob was rushing to finish the paper, his printer broke.

One way to tell whether the participle is dangling is to put the clause with the participle right after the subject of the sentence: "Bob's printer, rushing to finish the paper, broke." You can easily hear that it doesn't sound right.

Note: Not all words that end in *-ing* are participles. For example: "Completing the task by Tuesday is your next assignment." The word *completing* functions as a noun, not a verb. (Nouns ending in *-ing* are called *gerunds*.)

8. Misplaced modifiers

Incorrect: My parents bought a kitten for my sister they call Paws.

Correct: My parents bought a kitten they call Paws for my sister.

A *misplaced modifier* is a phrase, clause, or word placed too far from the noun or pronoun it describes. As a result, the sentence fails to convey your exact meaning. As this sentence is written, it means that the sister, not the kitten, is named Paws. That's because the modifier *they call Paws* is in the wrong place in the sentence. To correct a misplaced modifier, move the modifier as close as possible to the word or phrase it describes.

9. Incorrect idioms

Incorrect: It's raining cats and puppies.

Correct: It's raining cats and dogs.

The phrase "It's raining cats and dogs" is an *idiom,* an expression that has a figurative rather than literal meaning. Expressions such as "make a big deal out of it," "on the double," and "down and out" are idioms. If you decide to use idioms in your writing, be sure to use the correct phrase. For instance, it's idiomatic to say, "She talked *down* to him." It's not idiomatic to say, "She talked *under* to him."

Idiomatic prepositions are very common and just as hard to use. Here's a chart of the most useful ones:

Incorrect	Correct
according *with* the plan	according *to* the plan
accuse *with* perjury	accuse *of* perjury
apologize *about*	apologize *for*

Continues

Incorrect	Correct
board *of*	bored *with*
capable *to*	capable *of*
comply *to* the rules	comply *with* the rules
concerned *to*	concerned *about, over, with*
conform *in* standards	conform *to, with* standards
in search *for*	in search *of*
in accordance *to* policy	in accordance *with* policy
independent *from*	independent *of*
inferior *than* ours	inferior *to* ours
interested *about*	interested *in, by*
jealous *for* others	jealous *of* others
outlook *of* life	outlook *on* life
puzzled *on*	puzzled *at, by*
similar *with*	similar *to*

Quick Tip

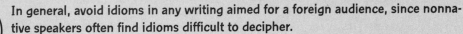

In general, avoid idioms in any writing aimed for a foreign audience, since nonnative speakers often find idioms difficult to decipher.

10. Biased language

   Incorrect: That old geezer is taking my parking space!

   Correct: That man is taking my parking space!

   Avoid language that denigrates people because of their age, gender, race, or physical condition. This is especially crucial in business, where such language could result in a lawsuit.

11. Incorrect voice (active versus passive voice)

   Passive voice: The meeting was attended by the executive.

   Active voice: The executive attended the meeting.

   As you learned in Chapter 3 in the section on active and passive voice, English has two voices: *active* and *passive*. A verb is *active* when the subject performs the action. A verb is *passive* when its action is performed upon the subject. The active voice is clearer and more concise than the passive voice.

   Even though the active voice is stronger than the passive voice, you should use the passive voice in these two situations:

- To avoid placing blame ("A mistake was made" rather than "You made a mistake.")
- To avoid identifying the doer of the action ("The letter was sent" rather than "Nicole sent the letter.")

Most Common Sentence Errors

12. Fragments (incomplete sentences)

     Fragment: If you want to be clearly understood.

     Correct: Don't write sentence fragments if you want to be clearly understood.

     Every sentence must have three things:

     - A subject: the "doer" of the action. The subject will be a noun or pronoun.
     - A verb: what the subject does.
     - A complete thought.

     The fragment in this example is missing a subject and a verb. As a result, the group of words does not express a complete thought. See Chapter 8 for a complete discussion of sentence fragments.

13. Run-ons (two sentences run together)

     Run-on: Daddy longlegs spiders are more poisonous than black widows, daddy longlegs spiders cannot bite humans because their jaws won't open wide enough.

     Correct: Daddy longlegs spiders are more poisonous than black widows, *but* daddy longlegs spiders cannot bite humans because their jaws won't open wide enough.

     or

     Daddy longlegs spiders are more poisonous than black widows; however, daddy longlegs cannot bite humans because their jaws won't open wide enough.

     A run-on sentence occurs when two complete sentences ("independent clauses") are incorrectly joined. Sentences can only be joined with a coordinating conjunction (*and, but, or, nor, for, so, yet*) or a semicolon—a comma doesn't cut the mustard. See Chapter 8 for a complete discussion of sentences.

Most Common Spelling Errors

Writers often misspell words because they mispronounce them. The three most common mistakes are

- Dropping a letter or syllable when we say a word.
- Adding an unnecessary letter when we say a word.
- Mispronouncing a word and so misspelling it.

14. Missing letters

     Here are 10 words that are frequently misspelled because the speaker drops a letter or syllable.

- *Accidentally:* The word has five syllables; drop one and *accidentally* becomes *accidently.*
- *Accompaniment:* The second *a* and the only *i* are the problems with *accompaniment.* To remember the *i,* you might want to use this mnemonic: there's a lot of *animal* in *accompaniment.*
- *Acreage:* The *e* presents the spelling problem because it is rarely stressed in speech. That's how people end up with *acrage.* It's also common for writers to misplace the *e,* as in *acerage.*
- *Anecdote:* Letters get dropped when writers mispronounce *anecdote* as *anedote.* Then there's *antidote*—a legitimate word, but the wrong one in context.
- *Asked:* This word gets mangled as *ast* or even *axed.* This results in such curious spellings as *askd, askt,* and *axst.*
- *Asterisk:* This word can end up spelled *aterisk, askterisk,* or even *acksterisk.*
- *Broccoli:* It's not hard to drop a *c* and add an *l* with this veggie. The correct pronunciation isn't going to do you much good here, so try breaking the word into two parts: *broc* and *coli.*
- *Calisthenics:* Stress the first *i* and the *e* to avoid dropping these letters when you spell *calisthenics.* Otherwise, you could end up with *calesthenics* or *calesthinics.*
- *Category:* Make sure to say that *e* as an *e* rather than an *a* to avoid the misspelling *catagory.*
- *Cemetery: Cemetary* is the result when the third *e* is pronounced as an *a.*

15. Extra letters

    Because of errors in pronunciation, spellers often insert an unnecessary vowel between two letters. Here are some of the most commonly misspelled words:

    - *Athlete:* Often mispronounced as *athalete,* resulting in that unnecessary *a.*
    - *Disastrous:* The word ends up with *disaster* stuck in there: *disasterous.* What extra letter do you see?
    - *Grievous:* Another common speech slip results in *grieveous* or *grievious.* No extra *e* or *i,* please.
    - *Hindrance:* This word falls prey to the same problem as *disastrous:* add *hinder* to *hindrance* and you get *hinderance.* Too many syllables!
    - *Lightning:* The bolt of electricity on a stormy night is often mispronounced and thus misspelled as *lightening.* Now, *lightening* is a legitimate word; it means that something is getting less dark. Say each letter to help you spell the word you want.
    - *Mischievous:* A surprising number of people mispronounce the word as *mischievious,* adding an extra *i.*
    - *Perseverance:* People often add an extra *r,* resulting in *perserverance.* Saying the word correctly will prevent this error.

Quick Tip

Long-time speakers and readers of English have learned basic connections between sounds and letter combinations that help them spell a large number of words. However, for historical reasons, certain combinations of letters are not always pronounced in the same way. For example, *ough* can be pronounced differently as in *thought, bough, through, drought.*

16. Transposed letters

    Mispronunciation can also result in scrambled letters. Here are some words especially prone to switched letters.

aesthetic	allegiance	analysis	analyze	anonymous
auxiliary	bureaucrat	diaphragm	entrepreneur	gasoline
gauge	gorgeous	irrelevant	khaki	lingerie
mileage	psychology	restaurant	rhyme	rhythm

17. Incorrect plurals

    Remember that *plural nouns* name more than one person, place, or thing. There are regular plurals and irregular ones. The regular plurals rarely result in spelling errors, but irregular plurals often cause trouble. Keep regular and irregular plurals straight and you'll eliminate a bunch of spelling errors. Below are some spelling rules to help you form the correct plurals.

    • Most regular plurals are formed by adding *s* to the end of the word.

Singular	Plural
bird	birds
hat	hats
arrow	arrows
pencil	pencils
duck	ducks
dog	dogs

- Add *es* if the noun ends in *s, sh, ch,* or *x.*

Singular	Plural
class	classes
inch	inches
box	boxes
stress	stresses
sex	sexes
tax	taxes
Jones	Joneses

- If the noun ends in *y* preceded by a *consonant,* change the *y* to *i* and add *es.*

Singular	Plural
city	cities
lady	ladies
happy	happiness
icy	iciness
activity	activities
cry	cries
blueberry	blueberries

- If the noun ends in *y* preceded by a *vowel,* add *s.*

Singular	Plural
essay	essays
monkey	monkeys
journey	journeys
survey	surveys
attorney	attorneys

Exception: Words that end in *-quy,* as in *soliloquy,* which becomes *soliloquies.*

- Words that end in *-ly* keep the *y* when they become plural.

Singular	Plural
bialy	bialys

- If the noun ends in *o* preceded by a *vowel*, add *s*.

Exceptions: dollies   lilies

Singular	Plural
radio	radios
ratio	ratios
patio	patios
studio	studios

- If the noun ends in *o* preceded by a *consonant*, the noun can take *es, s,* or either *s* or *es*.

	Singular	Plural
takes *es*	potato	potatoes
	hero	heroes
	tomato	tomatoes
	echo	echoes
	veto	vetoes
takes *s*	silo	silos
	solo	solos
	piano	pianos
	soprano	sopranos
	alto	altos
	dynamo	dynamos
either *es* or *s*	zero	zeros, zeroes
	tornado	tornados, tornadoes
	cargo	cargos, cargoes
	motto	mottos, mottoes
	domino	dominos, dominoes
	buffalo	buffalos, buffaloes

- Add *s* to most nouns ending in *f.* However, the *f* endings are so irregular as to be nearly random. If you have any doubts at all, consult a dictionary.

Singular	Plural
brief	briefs
chief	chiefs
proof	proofs
belief	beliefs
staff	staffs
sheriff	sheriffs
belief	beliefs

Exception: In some cases, change the *f* or *fe* to *v* and add *es:*

Singular	Plural
half	halves
knife	knives
leaf	leaves
life	lives
self	selves
thief	thieves
wife	wives
wolf	wolves

Exception: This rule doesn't hold for names. In that case, just add an *s:* Mr. and Ms. *Wolf* becomes The *Wolfs.*

- Words that end in *-ey, -ay,* or *-oy* do not have *-ies* plurals.

	Singular	Plural
-ey	valley	valleys
	abbey	abbeys
	jitney	jitneys
-ay	tray	trays
	clay	clays
-oy	ploy	ploys

- In compound words, make the main word plural.

Singular	Plural
mother-in-law	mothers-in-law
passerby	passersby
sister-in-law	sisters-in-law

Exceptions: If there is no noun in the compound word, add an *s* to the end of the word, as in *mix-ups, takeoffs.* If the compound word ends in *-ful,* add an *s* to the end of the word, as in *cupfuls.*

- Some nouns change their spelling when they become plural.

Singular	Plural
child	children
foot	feet
goose	geese
louse	lice
man	men
mouse	mice
ox	oxen
tooth	teeth
woman	women

- Some nouns have the same form whether they are singular or plural.

  swine   series   deer   sheep

  moose   species   Portuguese

- The only plurals formed with apostrophes are the plurals of numbers, letters, and words highlighted as words.

  How many 3's make 9? There were too many *but's* in the speech.

- Some words from other languages form plurals in other ways, often determined by the grammar of their language of origin.

Singular	Plural
alumnus	alumni (female)
alumna	alumnae (male)
analysis	analyses
axis	axes
bacterium	bacteria
basis	bases
crisis	crises
criterion	criteria
hypothesis	hypotheses
index	index, indices
memorandum	memorandums, memoranda
parenthesis	parentheses
phenomenon	phenomena
stimulus	stimuli
thesis	theses

18. Errors in confusing word pairs (such as *weather/whether*)

    Some words in English have the same spelling and pronunciation but different meanings, such as *bay/bay* and *beam/beam*. We also have words with the same pronunciation but different spellings and meanings, such as *coarse/course* or *bridal/bridle*. Distinguishing between these confusing words is crucial because it helps you write exactly what you mean.

    Below are some of the most often misspelled words. They're mangled because they're so close in sound and/or spelling. After you study the list, however, you'll be able to tell them apart and use them correctly.

    - *air:* atmosphere   There's no *air* in a vacuum—hence his empty head.

      err: make a mistake   To *err* is human; to purr, feline.

    - *a lot:* many   *A lot* of people are absent from work today.

      allot: divide   *Allot* the prizes equally among all guests, please.

    - *all together:* all at one time   The students spoke *all together.*

      altogether: completely   The job is *altogether* complete.

- *allowed:* given permission   You are *allowed* to vote for the candidate of your choice.
  aloud: out loud, verbally   Don't say it *aloud.* Don't even think it quietly.
- *already:* previously   We had *already* packed.
  all ready: prepared   The cole slaw is *all ready* to serve.
- *altar:* shrine   The priest placed the prayer book on the *altar.*
  alter: change   She had to *alter* her dress.
- *arc:* curved line   The walls have an *arc* rather than a straight line.
  ark: boat   Noah loaded the *ark* with animals.
- *are:* plural verb   Mae West said, "Brains *are* an asset, if you hide them."
  our: belonging to us   There's someone in the corner of *our* living room.
- *ascent:* to move up   She made a quick *ascent* up the corporate ladder!
  assent: to agree   I *assent* to your plan.
- *bare:* undressed   You can find a lot of *bare* people in nudist camps.
  bare: unadorned, plain   Just take the *bare* essentials when you go camping.
  bear: animal   Look at the *bear!*
  bear: carry, hold   I *bear* no grudges.
- *base:* the bottom part of an object, the plate in baseball, morally low
  The vase has a wide, sturdy *base.*
  The catcher's wild throw missed the *base.* The criminal is *base* and corrupt.
  bass: the lowest male voice, a type of fish, a musical instrument   He sings *bass.* We
  caught a striped *bass.* She plays the *bass* in the orchestra.
- *beau:* sweetheart   My *beau* bought me flowers.
  bow: to bend from the waist, a device used to propel arrows, loops of ribbon, the for
  ward end of a ship   The dancer liked to *bow* to his partner. We shoot deer with a
  bow and arrow. The baby wore a pretty hair *bow.* The passengers sat in the ship's *bow.*
- *board:* a slab of wood   The karate master cut the *board* with his bare hand.
  board: a group of directors   The school *board* meets the first Tuesday of every month.
  bored: not interested   The *movie* bored us so we left early.
- *born:* native   *Born* free . . . taxed to death.
  borne: endured   Fortunato had *borne* his insults the best he could.
- *bore:* tiresome person   What a *bore* he is!
  boar: male pig   They found a *boar* in the woods.
- *brake:* a device for slowing a vehicle   Use the car *brake!*
  break: to crack or destroy   Don't *break* my back.
- *breadth:* measurement   The desk has a *breadth* of more than 6 feet
  breath: inhale and exhale   She has bad *breath.*
- *capital:* the city or town that is the official seat of government, highly important, net
  worth of a business   Albany is the *capital* of New York state. What a *capital* idea!
  The business has $12 million operating *capital.*
  Capitol: the building in Washington, D.C., where the U.S. Congress meets   The
  Capitol is a beautiful building.
- *conscience:* moral sense   Your *conscience* helps you distinguish right from wrong.
  conscious: awake   Being *conscious:* that annoying time between naps.

- *cheep:* what a bird says   *"Cheep,"* said the canary.
  cheap: not expensive   Talk is *cheap* because supply exceeds demand.
- *deer:* animal   The *deer* sneered at the inept hunter.
  dear: beloved   "You are my *dear,"* the man said to his wife.
- *draft:* breeze   What's causing that *draft* on my neck?
  draft: sketch   Life: A first *draft,* with no rewrites.

Most Common Punctuation Errors

19. Missing commas or extra commas

    Incorrect: Avoid commas, that are not necessary.

    Correct: Avoid commas that are not necessary.

    Have you ever been advised to "add commas where you would take a breath"? Sometimes this advice works—but sometimes it doesn't. It's especially dangerous when you've gone over and over your writing. At that point, *nothing* looks correct. To avoid confusion and frustration, don't wing it. Instead, review the comma rules covered in Chapter 10. Use these rules as you write to help you correctly punctuate your documents.

20. Missing or misused apostrophes

    Incorrect: Save the apostrophe for it's proper use and omit it where its' not needed.

    Correct: Save the apostrophe for its proper use and omit it where it's not needed.

    As discussed in Chapter 10, the apostrophe (') is used in three ways: to show possession (ownership), to show plural forms, and to show contractions (where a letter or number has been omitted). The following chart shows how *its, it's,* and *its'* are used:

Word	Part of Speech	Meaning
it's	Contraction	It is
its	Possessive pronoun	Belonging to it
its'	Is not a word	None

21. Misused exclamation marks

    Incorrect: Of all U.S. presidents, none lived to be older than John Adams, who died at the age of 91!

    Correct: Of all U.S. presidents, none lived to be older than John Adams, who died at the age of 91.

    Never overuse exclamation marks. Instead of using exclamation marks, convey emphasis through careful, vivid word choice. Exclamation marks create an overwrought tone that often undercuts your point.

22. Misused semicolons

    Incorrect: Use the semicolon correctly always use it where it is appropriate; and never where it is not suitable.

Correct: Use the semicolon correctly; always use it where it is appropriate, and never where it is not suitable.

A semicolon has two primary uses: to separate two complete sentences ("independent clauses") whose ideas are closely related or to separate clauses that contain a comma. This is covered in detail in Chapter 10.

Most Common Capitalization Errors

23. Proper nouns not capitalized.

Incorrect: louisa adams, Wife of john quincy Adams, was the first (and only) foreign-born First Lady.

Correct: Louisa Adams, wife of John Quincy Adams, was the first (and only) foreign-born first lady.

Here are the basic rules of capitalization:

- *Capitalize all proper nouns.* These include names, geographical places, specific historical events, eras, and documents, languages, nationalities, countries, and races.
- *Capitalize the first word at the beginning of a sentence*

See Chapter 11 for a complete discussion of capitalization.

24. Errors in titles

Incorrect: *The Wind In The Willows*

Correct: *The Wind in the Willows*

Capitalize the major words in titles of books, plays, movies, newspapers, and magazines.

- Do not capitalize the articles: *a, an, the.*
- Do not capitalize prepositions: *at, by, for, of, in, up, on, so, on, to,* etc.
- Do not capitalize conjunctions: *and, as, but, if, or, nor.*

See Chapter 11 for a complete discussion of capitalization.

Most Common Proofreading Errors

25. Missing words

Incorrect: Proofread carefully to see if you have any words out.

Correct: Proofread carefully to see if you have *left* any words out.

This is a simple rule, but many people run out of time before they can proofread a document. *Always* make the time to proofread your writing. And try to let your writing sit and "cool off" for a few hours. The errors will become much more obvious and easier to isolate.

Improve Your Writing, One Step at a Time

How can you use the previous 25 guidelines to improve your writing? Try these ideas:

1. Don't try to master all the rules of grammar and usage at once; it's both futile and frustrating.

2. Instead, listen to the comments your readers mention when they discuss your writing.

3. Keep track of the writing errors you make by checking your own work against the guidelines. Review this checklist every time you write an important document. To isolate your most common writing errors, select several pieces of your writing, such as memos, letters, or reports.
   - Read the documents you selected for analysis several times.
   - Circle all the errors you find. Don't panic if you can't identify each type of error at this point. Just do the best you can.
   - Ask a friend or family member to read the documents and find additional errors.
   - Count up the number of errors in each category.
   - Reread the chapters that explain your specific writing problems.
   - Concentrate on these areas as you write.

4. Be patient. Learning the rules takes both time and effort. Remember that using standard grammar with confidence will help you build the credible image you want—and need.

It's a Wrap

✔ Correct grammar and usage are vital for educated professionals.

✔ Learn the rules of standard written English, but never let usage guidelines make your writing clumsy or obscure.

✔ Track your writing errors and concentrate on correcting the ones you make most often.

Test Yourself

QUESTIONS

True-False Questions

1. Long-winded writing may sound educated and impressive, but it actually turns off your audience because it wastes their time.

2. *Parallel structure* means that sentence parts match, singular to singular and plural to plural.

3. For a metaphor to be effective, it must compare images or objects that go together.

4. A modifier is said to "dangle" when the word it modifies has been left out of the sentence.

5. An *idiom* is a verb ending in *-ing*. Idioms always have literal meanings.

6. Never use language that denigrates people because of their age, gender, race, or physical condition.

7. Avoid the passive voice because the active voice is stronger and clearer.
8. A sentence fragment occurs when two complete sentences ("independent clauses") are incorrectly joined.
9. Writers often misspell words because they mispronounce them.
10. *Accidently* is spelled correctly.

Completion Questions

Select the word that best completes each sentence.

1. We add *-s* or *-es* to make the third-person *singular* form of most (nouns, verbs) but add *-s* or *es* to make the *plural* form of most (nouns, verbs).
2. (Redundancy, Metaphors) are figures of speech that compare two unlike things to explain the less-familiar object.
3. (A modifier, An idiom) is a word or phrase that describes a subject, verb, or object.
4. A (misplaced modifier, dangling construction) is a phrase, clause, or word placed too far from the noun or pronoun it describes. As a result, the sentence fails to convey your exact meaning
5. The word (baggy, sacrifice, exhaust, vegetable) is misspelled.
6. Because of errors in pronunciation, spellers often insert an unnecessary (modifier, vowel) between two letters.
7. (Their, There, They're) is a possessive word.
8. The (apostrophe, comma) is used to show possession and to show plural forms.
9. This mark of punctuation also shows (contraction, parallelism) where a letter or number has been omitted.
10. (Quotation marks, Exclamation marks) create an overwrought tone that often undercuts your point.

Multiple-Choice Questions

Choose the best answer to each question.

1. The following are all grammar and usage errors *except*
   (a) Incorrect idioms
   (b) Lack of parallel structure
   (c) Missing commas or extra commas
   (d) Dangling modifiers
2. The following are all classified as errors in mechanics *except*
   (a) Biased language
   (b) Missing or misused apostrophes
   (c) Missing commas or extra commas
   (d) Misused exclamation marks

3. Which is a run-on sentence?

    (a) Harry Truman's middle name was just S, but it isn't short for anything.

    (b) Harry Truman's middle name was just S, it isn't short for anything.

    (c) Harry Truman's middle name was just S; it isn't short for anything.

    (d) Harry Truman's middle name was just S, and it isn't short for anything.

4. Which is the best revision of the following sentence fragment:

Since Lincoln Logs were invented by Frank Lloyd Wright's son.

    (a) Because Lincoln Logs were invented by Frank Lloyd Wright's son.

    (b) When Lincoln Logs were invented by Frank Lloyd Wright's son.

    (c) After Lincoln Logs were invented by Frank Lloyd Wright's son.

    (d) Lincoln Logs were invented by Frank Lloyd Wright's son.

5. Which sentence is punctuated correctly?

    (a) Madison lived at Montpelier (tall mountain), Thomas Jefferson lived at Monticello (little mountain).

    (b) Madison, lived at Montpelier (tall mountain), Thomas Jefferson, lived at Monticello (little mountain).

    (c) Madison lived at Montpelier (tall mountain) Thomas Jefferson lived at Monticello (little mountain).

    (d) Madison lived at Montpelier (tall mountain); Thomas Jefferson lived at Monticello (little mountain).

6. Which sentence has a dangling modifier?

    (a) Coming up the hall, the clock struck ten.

    (b) As we came up the hall, the clock struck ten.

    (c) The clock struck ten when we came up the hall.

    (d) We heard the clock strike ten as we came up the hall.

7. Which sentence has a misplaced modifier?

    (a) Yesterday, the city police reported that two cars were stolen.

    (b) Two cars were reported stolen by the city police yesterday.

    (c) The city police reported yesterday that two cars were stolen.

    (d) The city police reported that two cars were stolen yesterday.

8. Which sentence is not parallel?

    (a) My date was obnoxious, loud, and cheap.

    (b) My date was obnoxious, loud, and tightfisted.

    (c) My date was obnoxious, loud, and didn't spend money easily.

    (d) My date was obnoxious, loud, and economical.

9. Every sentence must have all the following elements *except:*

    (a) A subject, a noun or pronoun

    (b) A modifier, an adjective or an adverb

    (c) A verb

    (d) A complete thought

10. Which of the following idioms is correct?
    (a) Outlook <u>on</u> life
    (b) In search <u>for</u>
    (c) Jealous <u>for</u> others
    (d) Puzzled <u>on</u>

Further Exercise

Correct all the errors in the following paragraph.

Sherlock holmes and watson camping in the forest. They gone to bed and were laying beneath the night sky. Holmes' said Whatson look up what do you see"

"I see thosands of stars."

"And what do that means to you? Holmes ask?

"I suppose it mean that of all the planets, in the universe, we are truly fortunate to be here on Earth. We are small in Gods eyes should struggle every day to be worthy of our blessings. In a meteorological sense it mean, well have a sunny day tomorow. What does it mean to you Holmes"

"To me it, means someone have stole our tent"

ANSWER KEY

True-False Questions

   1. T   2. F   3. T   4. T   5. F   6. T   7. F   8. F   9. T   10. F

Completion Questions

   1. verbs, nouns   2. Metaphors   3. A modifier   4. misplaced modifier
   5. vegetable   6. vowel   7. Their   8. apostrophe   9. contraction
   10. Exclamation marks

Multiple-Choice Questions

   1. c   2. a   3. b   4. d   5. d   6. a   7. b   8. c   9. b   10. a

Further Exercise

   Sherlock Holmes and Watson were camping in the forest. They had gone to bed and were lying beneath the night sky. Holmes said, "Watson, look up. What do you see?"

   "I see thousands of stars."

"And what does that mean to you?" Holmes asked.

"I suppose it means that of all the planets in the universe, we are truly fortunate to be here on Earth. We are small in God's eyes, but should struggle every day to be worthy of our blessings. In a meteorological sense, it means we'll have a sunny day tomorrow. What does it mean to you, Holmes?"

"To me, it means someone has stolen our tent."

PART 3

CHAPTER 7

Phrases and Clauses

Do I Need to Read This Chapter?

You should read this chapter if you need to review or learn about

➤ Prepositional phrases, appositives, and verbals

➤ The difference between independent and dependent clauses

➤ Adverb clauses, adjective clauses, relative clauses, and noun clauses

Get Started

This chapter opens with a discussion of the *phrase*, one of the key building blocks of the sentence. There are several different kinds of phrases, including prepositional phrases (with the subcategories adjectival phrases and adverbial phrases), appositives, and verbals. Then, you'll review the *clause*, a group of words with its own subject and verb.

Overview of Phrases

A *phrase* is a group of words that functions in a sentence as a single part of speech. A phrase does not have a subject or a verb, so it cannot stand alone as an independent unit—it can function only as a part of speech. As you write, you use phrases to add detail by describing. Phrases help you express yourself more clearly.

Type of Phrase	Definition	Examples
Prepositional	Begins with a preposition and ends with a noun or pronoun	near the house over the moon under the desk
Adjectival	Prepositional phrase that functions as an adjective	Marci has a scarf *with green stripes.*
Adverbial	Prepositional phrase that functions as an adverb	The fans shouted *with hoarse voices.*
Appositive	Noun or pronoun that renames another noun or pronoun	Fran, *a teacher,* enjoys summer vacation.
Verbal	Verb form used as another part of speech	See Participle, Gerund, Infinitive.
Participle	Verbal phrase that functions as an adjective	*Screaming loudly,* the baby was disconsolate.
Gerund	Verbal phrase that functions as a noun	*Working overtime* requires great sacrifice.
Infinitive	Verbal phrase that functions as a noun, adjective, or adverb	*To clean house on a spring day* is depressing.

Prepositional Phrases

A *prepositional phrase* is a group of words that begins with a preposition and ends with a noun or a pronoun. This noun or pronoun is called the "object of the preposition."

by the wall	near the closet	over the garage
with help	in the desert	below sea level

1. Adjectival phrases

   When a prepositional phrase serves as an adjective, it's called an *adjectival phrase.* An adjectival phrase, as with an adjective, describes a noun or a pronoun. To find out if a prepositional phrase is functioning as an adjectival phrase, see if it answers these questions: "Which one?" or "What kind?"

The *cost of the jeans* was surprisingly high.

The adjectival phrase "of the jeans" describes the noun *cost*.

The *clown with the mask* terrifies the children.

The adjectival phrase "with the mask" describes the noun *clown*.

2. Adverbial phrases

When a prepositional phrase serves as an adverb, it's called an *adverbial phrase*. In these cases, it describes a verb, an adjective, or adverb. To find out if a prepositional phrase is functioning as an adverbial phrase, see if it answers one of these questions: "Where?" "When?" "In what manner?" "To what extent?"

The Mets *played at Shea Stadium.*

The adverbial phrase "at Shea Stadium" modifies the verb *played.*

The game *lasted* into the fourteenth inning.

The adverbial phrase "into the fourteenth inning" modifies the verb *lasted.*

Appositives and Appositive Phrases

An *appositive* is a noun or a pronoun that renames another noun or pronoun. Appositives are placed directly after the nouns or pronouns they identify. *Appositive phrases* are nouns or pronouns with modifiers.

Lisa, *a friend,* should have understood my fear.

The appositive "a friend" renames the noun *Lisa.*

Tom's new car, *a PT Cruiser,* ran out of gas on the highway.

The appositive "a PT Cruiser" renames the noun *car.*

Lisa, *a dear old friend,* should have understood my fear.

The appositive phrase "a dear old friend" renames the noun *Lisa.*

Tom's new car, *a cherry red convertible PT Cruiser,* ran out of gas on the highway.

The appositive phrase "a cherry red convertible PT Cruiser" renames the noun *car.*

Verbal Phrases

A *verbal* is a verb form used as another part of speech. Verbals come in three varieties: *participles, gerunds,* and *infinitives.* Each type has a different function in a sentence:

- *Participles* function as adjectives.
- *Gerunds* function as nouns.
- *Infinitives* function as nouns, adjectives, or adverbs.

Although a verbal doesn't function as a verb in a sentence, it does retain two qualities of a verb:

- A verbal can be described by adverbs and adverbial phrases.
- A verbal can add modifiers to become a *verbal phrase.*

3. Participle phrases

A *participle* is a form of a verb that functions as an adjective. There are two kinds of participles: *present participles* and *past participles.*
- Present participles end in *-ing* (jumping, burning, speaking).
- Past participles usually end in *-ed, -t,* or *-en* (jumped, burnt, spoken).

The *wailing cats* disturbed the neighbors.

The present participle "wailing" describes the noun *cats.*

Annoyed, the *customer* stalked out of the store.

The past participle "annoyed" describes the noun *customer.*

Participle phrases contain a participle modified by an adverb or an adverbial phrase. They function as an adjective. A participle phrase can be placed before or after the word it describes.

Walking carefully, I avoided the spilled juice.

The participle phrase "walking carefully" describes the pronoun *I.*

Nina, bothered by the mess, cleaned it up.

The participle phrase "bothered by the mess" describes the noun *Nina.*

4. Gerund phrases

A *gerund* is a form of a verb used as a noun. *Gerunds* can function as subjects, direct objects, indirect objects, objects of a preposition, predicate nominative, and appositives.
- Gerunds always end in *-ing.*
- Gerunds always act as nouns.

In adult education, the Kitters discovered *dancing.*
The gerund "dancing" is a direct object.

Like a participle, a gerund can be part of a phrase.

The *slow, steady dripping* annoyed him.
The gerund phrase is "the slow, steady dripping."

Jill's morning schedule includes *exercising for a full hour.*
The gerund phrase is "exercising for a full hour."

Infinitive Phrases

The *infinitive* is a form of the verb that comes after the word *to* and acts as a noun, adjective, or adverb. An infinitive phrase contains modifiers that together act as a single part of speech.

His goal, *to get promoted before age 30,* didn't seem realistic.

The infinitive phrase "to get promoted before age 30" modifies the noun *goal*.

The honorees did not want *to attend the banquet in the evening.*

The infinitive phrase is "to attend the banquet in the evening."

Overview of Clauses

A *clause* is a group of words with its own subject and verb. Like phrases, clauses enrich your written and oral expression by adding details and making your meaning more exact. Clauses also allow you to combine ideas to show their relationship. This adds logic and cohesion to your speech and writing.

There are two types of clauses: *independent clauses* (main clauses) and *dependent clauses* (subordinate clauses and relative clauses).

- An *independent clause* is a complete sentence because it has a subject and verb and expresses a complete thought.
- A *dependent* (*subordinate*) *clause* is part of a sentence, so it cannot stand alone.

The following chart presents some examples.

Dependent Clause	Independent Clause
When opossums are playing 'possum,	they are not "playing."
In the great fire of London in 1666,	half of London was burnt down.
For a period of one year before an election,	all office-seekers in the Roman Empire were obliged to wear a certain white toga.

Dependent Clauses

Dependent clauses add additional information to the main clauses, but they are not necessary to complete the thought. Although each of the dependent clauses shown on the previous chart has a subject and a verb, it does not express a complete thought. As a result, it cannot stand alone.

A dependent clause often starts with a word that makes the clause unable to stand alone. Look back at the three dependent clauses in the chart on p. 102. The words used here are *when, in,* and *for,* respectively. These words are *subordinating conjunctions.*

Quick Tip

You can't determine whether a clause is independent or dependent from its length.

Either type of clause can be very long or very short—or somewhere in between. Skilled writers often vary the length of their clauses to achieve rhythm, balance, and meaning in their writing.

Subordinating conjunctions link an independent clause to a dependent clause. Each subordinating conjunction expresses a relationship between the dependent clause and the independent clause. For example, some conjunctions show time order, while others show result or effect.

The following chart lists the subordinating conjunctions used most often and the relationships they express:

Subordinating Conjunctions	Relationship
unless, provided that, if, even if	Condition
because, as, as if	Reason
rather than, than, whether	Choice
though, although, even though, but	Contrast
where, wherever	Location
in order that, so, so that, that	Result, effect
while, once, when, since, as whenever, after, before, until, as soon	Time

Quick Tip

When a dependent clause introduced by a subordinating conjunction comes *before* the independent clause, the clauses are usually separated by a comma.

When you are in Greece, you should visit the Parthenon.
(before)
You should visit the Parthenon when you are in Greece.
(after)

There are three different kinds of subordinate clauses: *adverb clauses, adjective clauses,* and *noun clauses.*

1. Adverb clause

   An *adverb clause* is a dependent clause that describes a verb, adjective, or other adverb. As with adverbs, an adverb clause answers these questions:

   Where? Why? When?

   To what extent? Under what condition? In what manner?

   You can place an adverb clause in the beginning, middle, or end of a sentence.

   - Adverb clause at the beginning of a sentence:

     Wherever Misty goes, she *leaves* broken hearts behind.

     The adverb clause "wherever she goes" modifies the verb *leaves.*

   - Adverb clause in the middle of a sentence:

     Fritz liked the meal *more than Tish did* because she is a picky eater.

     The adverb clause "than Tish did" modifies the adverb *more.*

   - Adverb clause at the end of a sentence:

     Harvey wanted to *change* his appearance *because he was wanted for embezzlement.*

     The adverb clause "because he was wanted for embezzlement" modifies the verb *change.*

2. Adjective clauses

   An adjective clause is a dependent clause that describes nouns and pronouns. As with adjectives, an adjective clause answers these questions:

   What kind? Which one? How many? How much?

   Most adjective clauses start with the pronouns *who, whom, why, whose, which, that, when, where.*

   The *traffic* is never light on the days *when I'm in a hurry.*

   The adjective clause "when I'm in a hurry" describes the noun *traffic.*

   We selected the *candidates* who were best qualified for the job.

   The adjective clause "who were best qualified for the job" describes the noun *candidates.*

3. Relative clauses

   Adjective clauses that begin with one of the relative pronouns are called *relative clauses.* The relative pronouns are: *who, whom, whose, which, that.* Relative pronouns connect an adjective clause to the word the clause describes.

   Ms. Harris, whose son is an athlete, is used to having their home filled with sporting equipment.

   The relative clause "whose son is an athlete" describes the noun *Ms. Harris.*

   The person *of whom you spoke* is my cousin.

   The relative clause "of whom you spoke" describes the noun *person.*

Quick Tips

Use *who, whom* (and all variations such as *whoever* and *whomever*) to refer to people. Use *which* and *that* if the antecedent is a thing or an animal.

4. Noun clauses

A noun clause is a dependent clause that functions as a noun.

Tracey does *whatever her parents ask her to do.*

The noun clause is "whatever her parents ask her to do."

The teacher did not accept my excuse *that the dog ate my homework.*

The noun clause is "that the dog ate my homework."

It's a Wrap

✔ A *phrase* is a group of words, without a subject or a verb, that functions as a single part of speech. Phrases cannot stand alone as an independent unit.

✔ *Prepositional phrases* begin with a preposition and end with a noun or pronoun; they can function as *adjectival phrases* and *adverbial phrases.*

✔ *Appositives* rename another noun or pronoun; *appositive phrases* include modifiers.

✔ *Verbals* are verb forms used as another part of speech. *Participles* function as adjectives; *gerunds* function as nouns; *infinitives* function as nouns, adjectives, or adverbs.

✔ An *independent (main) clause* is a complete sentence.

✔ A *dependent (subordinate) clause* is part of a sentence; it cannot stand alone.

Test Yourself

QUESTIONS

True-False Questions

1. A *phrase* is a group of words that functions in a sentence as a single part of speech.

2. A phrase has a subject and a verb, so it can stand alone as an independent unit.

3. A *prepositional phrase* is a group of words that begins with a preposition and ends with a noun or a pronoun.

4. The italic portion of the following sentence is a prepositional phrase:
   Frisky, *my loyal Irish setter,* can always sense when I'm upset.

5. An *adjectival phrase* describes a noun or a pronoun.

6. To find out if a prepositional phrase serves as an adjectival phrase, see if it answers these questions: "In what manner?" or "To what extent?"

7. The italic portion of the following sentence is functioning as an adjective phrase:
   The fireworks continued *late into the night.*

8. *Adverbial phrases* describe a verb, an adjective, or adverb.

9. The italic portion of the following sentence is functioning as an adverbial phrase: The Little League team competed *in the local arena.*

10. A *clause* is a noun or a pronoun that renames another noun or pronoun.

11. A *verbal* is a verb form used as another part of speech.

12. Verbals are the same as appositives.

13. *Participles* function as adjectives.

14. *Infinitives* function as nouns.

15. *Gerunds* function as nouns, adjectives, or adverbs.

16. Present participles always end in *-ing* (kissing, leaping, moaning).

17. Past participles often end in *-ed, -t,* or *-en* as in *smoked* and *burnt.*

18. Gerunds always end in *-ing* and function as verbs.

19. The italic phrase in the following sentence is an infinitive:
Why did the chicken cross the road?
To Ernest Hemingway: <u>*To die*</u>. In the rain.

20. The italic portion of the following sentence is functioning as an adjectival clause:
I met a woman *who works with your uncle.*

21. The italic portion of the following sentence is functioning as an adjectival clause:
Whenever he travels, Steve collects souvenirs.

22. The italic portion of the following sentence is functioning as an adverbial clause:
He ran *as if he had a torn ligament.*

23. The italic portion of the following sentence is functioning as an adverbial clause:
Whomever you hire must speak Spanish.

24. The italic portion of the following sentence is functioning as a noun clause:
The big question is *whether she will be able to attend the meeting.*

25. The italic portion of the following sentence is functioning as an independent clause:
Before they invented drawing boards, what did they go back to?

Completion Questions

Select the word that best completes each sentence.

1. A *clause* is a group of words with its own subject and (relative pronoun, verb).

2. There are two types of clauses: independent clauses and (verbal clauses, dependent clauses).

3. Independent clauses are also called (main clauses, relative clauses).

4. (Adjectival, Subordinating) conjunctions link an independent clause to a dependent clause.

5. The conjunction *unless* shows (time, condition).

6. The conjunction *although* shows (contrast, result).

7. Dependent clauses are the same as (infinitives, subordinate clauses).

8. All dependent clauses are (subordinate clauses, complete sentences).

9. When a dependent clause introduced by a subordinating conjunction comes before the independent clause, the clauses are usually separated by a (comma, colon).

10. As with adverbs, an adverb clause answers these questions: Where? Why? When? (In what manner? What kind?).

11. Adjective clauses that begin with one of the relative pronouns are called (prepositional, relative) clauses.

12. The relative pronouns are: *who, whom, whose, which,* (*that, there*).

13. Use *which* and *that* if the antecedent is a (person, thing).

14. The following word group is a (dependent, independent) clause:
    If the no. 2 pencil is the most popular, why is it still no. 2?

15. The following italic word group is a (dependent, independent) clause:
    If most car accidents occur within 5 miles of home, *why doesn't everyone just move 10 miles away?*

Multiple-Choice Questions
Choose the best answer to each question.

1. Which of the following is *not* a prepositional phrase?
   (a) By the desk
   (b) In the rearview mirror
   (c) Over their heads
   (d) That he didn't invite his relatives to the party

2. What is the adjectival phrase in this sentence?
   Put that box of heavy books on the counter, please.
   (a) Of heavy books
   (b) Put that box
   (c) Please
   (d) On the counter

3. What is the adverbial phrase in this sentence?
   The hang glider soared over the cool green lake.
   (a) The hang glider
   (b) Soared
   (c) Over the cool green lake
   (d) Cool green lake

4. All the following are subordinating conjunctions *except*
   (a) After
   (b) Walks

(c) Because

(d) Unless

5. Most adjective clauses start with the pronouns *who, whom, why, whose, which, that, when,* or

    (a) *Since*

    (b) *Where*

    (c) *Because*

    (d) *However*

6. What is the prepositional phrase in the following sentence?
   The hotel on the beach is always crowded.

    (a) The hotel

    (b) Is always crowded

    (c) On the beach

    (d) The beach is

7. What is the appositive in the following sentence?
   The expressway, built in 1950 with federal funds, is badly in need of repair.

    (a) The expressway

    (b) Is badly in need

    (c) Of repair

    (d) Built in 1950 with federal funds

8 What is the participle phrase in the following sentence?
   The toast, thoroughly burnt, sent a foul odor through the house, but Skip ate it anyway.

    (a) The toast

    (b) Thoroughly burnt

    (c) Sent a foul odor through the house

    (d) But Skip ate it anyway

9. What is the independent clause in this sentence?
   If work is so terrific, how come they have to pay you to do it?

    (a) How come they have to pay you to do it

    (b) If work is so terrific

    (c) How come they have

    (d) To pay you to do it

10. What is the dependent clause in this sentence?
    If all the world is a stage, where is the audience sitting?

    (a) If all the world is a stage

    (b) If all the world

    (c) Is a stage

    (d) Where is the audience sitting

11. What is the italic word group in the following sentence called?
    Our house, *shaded completely by old trees,* stays cool in the summer.
    (a) Independent clause
    (b) Prepositional phrase
    (c) Participle clause
    (d) Participle phrase

12. What is the italic word group in the following sentence called?
    Waiting for the train exhausted her patience.
    (a) Noun clause
    (b) Gerund phrase
    (c) Prepositional phrase
    (d) Independent clause

13. What is the italic word group in the following sentence called?
    The visitors forgot *to give their address.*
    (a) Prepositional phrase
    (b) Infinitive clause
    (c) Infinitive phrase
    (d) Prepositional clause

14. What is the italic word group in the following sentence called?
    If you ate pasta and antipasta, would you still be hungry?
    (a) Dependent phrase
    (b) Independent clause
    (c) Dependent clause
    (d) Independent phrase

15. What is the italic word group in the following sentence called?
    Hermione wanted her name changed *because it was hard to pronounce.*
    (a) Adverb clause
    (b) Adverb phrase
    (c) Infinitive phrase
    (d) Sentence

ANSWER KEY

True-False Questions

1. T   2. F   3. T   4. F   5. T   6. F   7. F   8. T   9. T   10. F   11. T   12. F
13. T   14. F   15. F   16. T   17. T   18. F   19. T   20. T   21. F   22. T
23. F   24. T   25. F

Completion Questions

1. verb   2. dependent clauses   3. main clauses   4. Subordinating   5. condition
6. contrast   7. subordinate clauses   8. subordinate clauses   9. comma
10. In what manner?   11. relative   12. that   13. thing   14. dependent
15. independent

Multiple-Choice Questions

1. d   2. a   3. c   4. b   5. b   6. c   7. d   8. b   9. a   10. a   11. d   12. b
13. c   14. c   15. a

CHAPTER 8

Writing Correct and Complete Sentences

You should read this chapter if you need to review or learn about

→ Identifying sentences

→ The four sentence functions

→ The four sentence forms

→ Identifying and correcting run-on sentences

→ Identifying and correcting sentence fragments and comma splices

Get Started

Here we will focus on sentences and sentence parts masquerading as sentences. First, you will discover how to identify sentences by their function and form. Then you will practice correcting incomplete and incorrect sentences.

What is a Sentence?

Sentence: Halt!

Sentence: You halt!

Sentence: Please halt right now, before you go any further.

Each of these three word groups is a sentence because they each meet the three requirements for a sentence. To be a sentence, a group of words must

- Have a *subject* (noun or pronoun)
- Have a *predicate* (verb or verb phrase)
- Express a *complete thought*

A *sentence* has two parts: a *subject* and a *predicate*. The *subject* includes the noun or pronoun that tells what the subject is about. The *predicate* includes the verb that describes what the subject is doing.

Subject	Predicate
(*You* is understood but unstated)	Halt!
Age	is the outrageous price paid for maturity.
A crocodile	cannot stick its tongue out.
Several tourists	are lost in the winding roads of Corfu.
Some toothpastes	contain antifreeze.

Therefore, a sentence is a group of words with two main parts: a subject area and a predicate area. Together, the subject and predicate express a complete thought.

Being able to recognize the subject and the verb in a sentence will help you make sure that your own sentences are complete and clear. To check that you've included the subject and verb in your sentences, follow these steps:

- To find the subject, ask yourself, "What word is the sentence describing?"
- To find an action verb, ask yourself, "What did the subject do?"
- If you can't find an action verb, look for a linking verb.

Quick Tip

In a question, the verb often comes before the subject. For example: "Is the ice cream in the freezer?" The verb is *is;* the subject is *ice cream.*

The Four Different Sentence Functions

In addition to classifying sentences by the number of clauses they contain, we can pigeonhole sentences according to their function. There are four sentence functions in English: *declarative, exclamatory, interrogative,* and *imperative.*

1. *Declarative sentences* state an idea. They end with a period.
   Grasshoppers contain more than 60 percent protein.
   Insects are rich in necessary vitamins and minerals.
   Crickets are packed with calcium, a mineral crucial for bone growth.
   Termites and caterpillars are a rich source of iron.

2. *Exclamatory sentences* show strong emotions. They end with an exclamation mark.
   I can't believe you left the car at the station overnight!
   What a mess you made in the kitchen!
   Our evening is ruined!
   The china is smashed!

3. *Interrogative sentences* ask a question. They end with a question mark.
   Who would eat bugs?
   Where did you put the eraser?
   Would you please help me with this package?
   What do you call this dish?

4. *Imperative sentences* give orders or directions, and so end with a period or an exclamation mark. Imperative sentences often omit the subject, as in a command.
   Take this route to save 5 miles.
   Clean up your room!
   Sit down and listen!
   Fasten your seatbelts when the sign is illuminated.

The Four Different Sentence Types

In Chapter 7, you reviewed independent and dependent clauses. These word groups can be used in a number of ways to form the four basic types of sentences: *simple, compound, complex, compound-complex.* Let's look at these sentence types now.

1. Simple sentences

    A *simple sentence* has one independent clause. That means it has one subject and one verb—although either or both can be compound. In addition, a simple sentence can have adjectives and adverbs. What a simple sentence can't have is another independent clause or any subordinate clauses.

    The *snow   melted* quickly in the bright sunshine.
        subject   verb

    Oprah Winfrey and *Conan O'Brien host* talk shows.
        subject   subject   verb

    The *flower bent* in the wind but did not *break.*
        subject verb   verb

    Both the *students* and the *teachers cheered* and *clapped* for the winning team.
            subject   subject   verb   verb

    Just because a simple sentence seems "simple" doesn't mean that it isn't powerful. It is. For instance, Noble Prize-winning author Ernest Hemingway crafted a powerful style using mainly simple sentences. In the following excerpt from his book *A Farewell to Arms,* Hemingway uses the simple sentence to convey powerful emotions. The simple sentences are in italic:

    > *My knee wasn't there.* My hand went in and my knee was down to my shin. *Passini was dead. That left three.* Someone took hold of me under the arms and someone else lifted up my legs.
    >
    > *"There are three others," I said. "One is dead."*
    >
    > *"It's Manera.* We went for a stretcher but there wasn't any. *How are you, Tenente?"*
    >
    > *"Where are Gordini and Gavuzzi?"*
    >
    > *"Gordini's at the post getting bandaged. Gavuzzi has your legs. Hold on to my neck, Tenente. Are you badly hit?"*

2. Compound sentences

    A *compound sentence* has two or more independent clauses. The independent clauses can be joined in one of two ways:

    - With a coordinating conjunction: *for, and, nor, but, or, yet, so*
    - With a semicolon (;)

    As with a simple sentence, a compound sentence can't have any subordinate clauses.

Insect cuisine may not be standard food in the United States, indep. clause	but conj.	*Science World* notes that 80 percent of the world's population savors bugs. indep. clause
Grasshoppers are the most commonly consumed insect, indep. clause	yet conj.	wasps have the highest protein of all edible insects. indep. clause
The car is unreliable indep. clause	; semicolon	it never starts in the rain. indep. clause

You may also add a conjunctive adverb to this construction. The following words are conjunctive adverbs:

accordingly	afterall	again	also
besides	consequently	finally	for example
for instance	furthermore	however	indeed
moreover	nevertheless	nonetheless	notwithstanding
on the other hand	otherwise	regardless	still
then	therefore	though	thus

The sentence construction looks like this:

independent clause; conjunctive adverb, independent clause

Grasshoppers eat clean plants;	however,	lobsters eat foul materials.
indep. clause	conj. adv.	indep. clause
Nico worked hard;	therefore	she got a merit raise.
indep. clause	conj. adv.	indep. clause

Quick Tip

Don't join the two parts of a compound sentence with a comma because you will end up with a type of run-on sentence called a *comma splice*. More on this later in this chapter.

3. Complex sentences

A *complex sentence* contains one independent clause and at least one dependent clause. The independent clause is called the *main clause*. These sentences use *subordinating conjunctions* to link ideas. The subordinating conjunctions include such words as: *because, as, as if, unless, provided that, if, even if.* A complete list of subordinating conjunctions appears in Chapter 7.

Since insects don't have much muscle,	their texture is similar to that of a clam.
dep. clause	indep. clause
No one answered	when he called the house.
indep. clause	dep. clause
It was no secret	that he was very lazy.
indep. clause	dep. clause

4. Compound-complex sentences

A *compound-complex sentence* has at least two independent clauses and at least one dependent clause. The dependent clause can be part of the independent clause.

When the drought comes,	the reservoirs dry up,	and residents know that water restrictions will be in effect.
dep. clause	indep. clause	indep. clause
Chris wanted to drive to work, indep. clause	but she couldn't indep. clause	until her car was repaired. dep. clause

Choosing Sentence Types

You now have four different types of sentences to use as you craft your ideas into language: simple sentences, compound sentences, complex sentences, and compound-complex sentences. Which ones should you use?

Should you write mainly simple sentences, as Ernest Hemingway did? Perhaps you should use complex sentences, favored by Charles Dickens and William Faulkner. Consider the Big Three—*purpose, audience,* and *subject*—as you craft your sentences:

- *Purpose.* Always consider your purpose for writing before you select a sentence type. Are you trying to entertain, persuade, tell a story, or describe? Sentences that describe are often long, while those that persuade may be much shorter. However, this guideline isn't firm: The length and complexity of your sentences also depends on your audience, topic, and personal style.

- *Audience.* Your choice of sentences also depends on your audience. For example, the more sophisticated your audience, the longer and more complex your sentences can be. Conversely, the less sophisticated your audience, the shorter and simpler your sentences should be.

- *Subject.* Your choice of sentence types also depends on your subject matter. The more complex your ideas, the simpler your sentences should be. This helps your audience grasp your ideas.

Overall, most effective sentences are concise, conveying their meaning in as few words as possible. Effective sentences stress the main point or the most important detail. This ensures that your readers understand your point. Most writers—professional as well as amateur—use a combination of all four sentence types to convey their meaning.

Quick Tip

No matter which sentence form you select, remember that every sentence must provide clear and complete information.

Sentence Errors: Run-on Sentences and Comma Splices

There are two basic types of sentence errors: *fragments* and *run-on sentences*. These problems with sentence construction confuse your readers and obscure your meaning. Their use will also result in clumsy, unpolished writing and speech. Let's look at each of these sentence errors in detail so that you'll be able to fix them with ease.

As you've learned, there are two types of clauses: *independent* and *dependent*.

- *Independent clauses* are complete sentences because they have a subject, a verb, and express a complete thought.

   I go to the movies every Saturday night.

   Richard Nixon's favorite drink was a dry martini.

- *Dependent clauses* cannot stand alone because they do not express a complete thought, even though they have a subject and a verb.

   Since   *I*   *enjoy* the movies.
      subject. verb

   Because Richard Nixon's favorite   *drink*   *was*   a dry martini.
               subject.   verb

A *run-on sentence* is two incorrectly joined independent clauses. A *comma splice* is a run-on sentence with a comma where the two independent clauses run together. When your sentences run together, your ideas are garbled.

Run-on: Our eyes are always the same size from birth our nose and ears never stop growing.

Corrected: Our eyes are always the same size from birth, *but* our nose and ears never stop growing.

Run-on: A duck's quack doesn't echo, no one knows why.

Corrected: A duck's quack doesn't echo; no one knows why.

or

A duck's quack doesn't echo, *and* no one knows why.

Run-on: The traditional sonnet has 14 lines, 10 syllables make up each line.

Corrected: The traditional sonnet has 14 lines; 10 syllables make up each line.

or

The traditional sonnet has 14 lines, *and* 10 syllables make up each line.

Quick Tip

Run-on sentences are not necessarily long. Some can be quite short, in fact. Mary fell asleep John left. Nick cooked Rita cleaned up.

You can correct a run-on sentence in four ways. Let's use the following example.

Water and wind are the two main causes of erosion, they constantly change the appearance of the Earth.

1. Divide the run-on sentence into two sentences with the appropriate end punctuation, such as a period, exclamation mark, or a question mark.

   Water and wind are the two main causes of erosion. They constantly change the appearance of the Earth.

2. Add a coordinating conjunction (*and, nor, but, or, for, yet, so*) to create a compound sentence.

   Water and wind are the two main causes of erosion, *for* they constantly change the appearance of the Earth.

3. Add a subordinating conjunction to create a complex sentence.

   Since water and wind are the two main causes of erosion, they constantly change the appearance of the Earth.

4. Use a semicolon to create a compound sentence.

   Water and wind are the two main causes of erosion; they constantly change the appearance of the Earth.

Here's what the sentence looks like with a conjunctive adverb added:

Water and wind are the two main causes of erosion; *as a result,* they constantly change the appearance of the Earth.

Which corrected version do you choose? Select the one that best suits your audience, purpose, and writing style. Ask yourself these questions as you decide:

- Which version will my readers like best?
- Which version will most clearly and concisely communicate my message?
- Which version fits best with the rest of the passage?

Sentence Errors: Fragments

As its name suggests, a *sentence fragment* is a group of words that do not express a complete thought. Most times, a fragment is missing a subject, a verb, or both. Other times, a fragment may have a subject and a verb but still not express a complete thought. Fragments can be phrases as well as clauses.

Quick Tip

Sentence fragments are common and acceptable in speech, but not in writing—unless you are recreating dialogue in a short story or novel.

There are three main ways that fragments occur.

1. Fragments occur when a dependent clause masquerades as a sentence.
   Because more and more teenagers are staying up far too late.
   Since they do not compensate for the sleep they miss.

2. Fragments also happen when a phrase is cut off from the sentence it describes.
   Used to remove a wide variety of stains on carpets and upholstery.
   Trying to prevent the new cotton shirt from shrinking in the dryer.

3. You can also create a fragment if you use the wrong form of a verb.
   The frog *gone* to the pond by the reservoir.
   Saffron *being* a very costly and pungent spice.

Quick Tip

Don't be misled by a capital letter at the beginning of a word group. Starting a group of words with a capital letter doesn't make the word group a sentence. It just makes it a fragment that starts with a capital letter.

You can correct a fragment three ways:

1. Add the missing part to the sentence.

   Fragment: Because more and more teenagers are staying up far too late.

   Complete: Because more and more teenagers are staying up far too late, they are sleep deprived.

   Fragment: Since they do not compensate for the sleep they miss.

   Complete: Since they do not compensate for the sleep they miss, teenagers often get cranky in the afternoon.

Fragment: Used to remove a wide variety of stains on carpets and upholstery.

Complete: This product is used to remove a wide variety of stains on carpets and upholstery.

Fragment: Trying to prevent the new cotton shirt from shrinking in the dryer.

Complete: Jean was trying to prevent the new cotton shirt from shrinking in the dryer.

2. Correct the misused verb.

Fragment: The frog *gone* to the pond by the reservoir.

Complete: The frog *went* to the pond by the reservoir.

Fragment: Saffron *being* a very costly and pungent spice.

Complete: Saffron *is* a very costly and pungent spice.

3. Omit the subordinating conjunction or connect it to another sentence.

Fragment: *Because* more and more teenagers are staying up far too late.

Complete: More and more teenagers are staying up far too late.

Fragment: *Since* they do not compensate for the sleep they miss.

Complete: They do not compensate for the sleep they miss.

It's a Wrap

✔ A *sentence* has a subject, a verb, and expresses a complete thought.

✔ The four sentence functions are *declarative, exclamatory, interrogative, imperative.*

✔ The four types of sentences are *simple, compound, complex, compound-complex.*

✔ *Run-on sentences* are incorrectly joined independent clauses; *fragments* are parts of sentences. Both are considered incorrect in formal written speech (although fragments are often used in written dialogue).

Test Yourself

QUESTIONS

True-False Questions

1. A *sentence* has two parts: a *subject* and a *predicate*.

2. The *predicate* includes the noun or pronoun that tells what the subject is about. The *subject* includes the verb that describes what the subject is doing.

3. Together, the subject and predicate express a complete thought.

4. In a question, the verb often comes after the subject.

5. *Declarative sentences* state an idea. They end with a period.

6. The following is a declarative sentence:

   Antonia ('Tonie') Nathan, the 1972 vice-presidential candidate of the Libertarian party, was the first woman in American history to receive an electoral vote.

7. *Exclamatory sentences* ask a question. They end with a question mark.

8. The following is an exclamatory sentence:

   What career did Ronald Reagan have before he became president?

9. *Interrogative sentences* give orders or directions, and so end with a period or an exclamation mark.

10. The following is an interrogative sentence:

    Where did you put my mink coat?

11. *Imperative sentences* give orders or directions, and so end with a period or an exclamation mark.

12. The following is an imperative sentence:

    Extinguish all smoking material while the sign is lit.

13. A *simple sentence* has two or more independent clauses.

14. The following is a simple sentence:

    When the Hoovers did not want to be overheard by White House guests, they spoke to each other in Chinese.

15. A *compound sentence* has two or more independent clauses.

16. The following is a compound sentence.

    Andrew Johnson, the seventeenth president, was the only self-educated tailor ever to serve as president.

17. Don't join the two parts of a compound sentence with a comma because you will end up with a type of run-on sentence called a "comma splice."

18. The following is a run-on sentence:

    Julie Nixon, daughter of Richard Nixon, married David Eisenhower, son of Dwight D. Eisenhower.

19. The following is a run-on sentence:

    William Henry Harrison was the first president to die in office, he was the oldest president ever elected.

20. The following sentence is a fragment:

    Ronald Reagan and his wife Nancy Davis opposite each other in the movie *Hellcats of the Navy.*

Completion Questions

Select the word that best completes each sentence.

1. Effective sentences stress the (minor, main) point or the most important detail.

2. A run-on sentence is the same as a (fragment, comma splice).

3. There are two basic types of sentence errors: *fragments* and (*run-on sentences, independent clauses*).

4. (*Dependent, Independent*) *clauses* are complete sentences because they have a subject and a verb and express a complete thought.

5. (*Dependent, Independent*) *clauses* cannot stand alone because they do not express a complete thought, even though they have a subject and a verb.

6. You can join the clauses in a compound sentence with a coordinating conjunction or a (semicolon, preposition).

7. The word (nonetheless, and) is a conjunctive adverb.

8. A *complex sentence* contains one independent clause and at least one (dependent clause, adjective).

9. The independent clause in a complex sentence is called the ("subordinate clause," "main clause").

10. A *compound-complex sentence* has at least two (independent, short) clauses and at least one dependent clause.

11. In a *compound-complex sentence,* the dependent clause (cannot, can) be part of the independent clause.

12. The length and complexity of your sentences depends on your audience, topic, and (personal style, readers).

13. The more complex your ideas, the (more difficult, simpler) your sentences should be.

14. Overall, most effective sentences are (concise, verbose), conveying their meaning in as few words as possible.

15. Fragments also happen when a phrase is (added to, cut off from) the sentence it describes.

Multiple-Choice Questions
Choose the best answer to each question.

1. To be a sentence, a group of words must have all the following *but*
    (a) (A subject
    (b) An adjective
    (c) A verb
    (d) A complete thought

2. The four sentence functions in English include all the following *except*
    (a) Declarative
    (b) Exclamatory
    (c) Declining
    (d) Interrogative

3. Which of the following sentences is best classified as exclamatory?

(a) People in Bali remove the wings from dragonflies and boil the bodies in coconut milk and garlic.

(b) The birds in my yard help keep the insect population under control.

(c) Look at that gorgeous insect on the fence!

(d) Would you eat insects?

4. Which of the following sentences is interrogative?

(a) A new language can come into being as a pidgin.

(b) A pidgin is a makeshift jargon containing words of various languages and little in the way of grammar.

(c) The leap into a "true" language is made when the pidgin speakers have children!

(d) Is language innate in humans?

5. Which of the following is *not* a declarative sentence?

(a) Venezuelans like to feast on fresh fire-roasted tarantulas.

(b) Eating insects is disgusting!

(c) In Japan, gourmets relish aquatic fly larvae sauteed in sugar and soy sauce.

(d) Many South Africans adore fried termites with cornmeal porridge.

6. When you are deciding which sentence types to use, consider all the following factors *except*

(a) Purpose

(b) Your handwriting

(c) Audience

(d) Subject

7. Which of the following is a simple sentence?

(a) The "ZIP" in zip code stands for "zone improvement plan."

(b) Lyndon Johnson loved the soda Fresca so much he had a fountain installed in the Oval Office that dispensed the beverage, which the president could operate by pushing a button on his desk chair.

(c) There was some question as to whether Barry Goldwater could legally serve as president because the Constitution requires presidents to be born in the United States and Goldwater was born in Arizona before it was a state.

(d) Despite being only five stories high, the Pentagon is one of the biggest office buildings in the world.

8. Which of the following is a compound sentence?

(a) Sirimauo Bandranaike of Sri Lanka became the world's first popularly elected female head of state in 1960.

(b) Andrew Jackson was the only U.S. president who believed that the world was flat.

(c) Six-time Socialist party candidate for President of the United States Norman

Thomas never polled more than 884,000 popular votes in one election, but his influence on American political and social thought was very effective.

(d) The first U.S. president to ride in an automobile was William McKinley.

9. Which of the following is a complex sentence?

   (a) George Washington's false teeth were made of whale bone.

   (b) George Washington was deathly afraid of being buried alive.

   (c) Washington's second inaugural address was 138 words long.

   (d) If children are capable of creating grammar without any instruction, then such grammar must preexist in their brains.

10. Which of the following is a compound-complex sentence?

   (a) When President Franklin Pierce ran down an elderly woman, the charges against him could not be proven, and the case was dismissed.

   (b) When George Washington was elected president, there was a king in France, a czarina in Russia, an emperor in China, and a shogun in Japan.

   (c) George Washington had to borrow money to go to his own inauguration.

   (d) James K. Polk was the only president to have been Speaker of the House.

11. Which word group is a fragment?

   (a) The Pentagon has more than 3 million square feet of office space it can house about 30,000 employees.

   (b) Theodore Roosevelt's wife and mother dying on the same day.

   (c) Currently, there are more handwritten letters from George Washington than from John F. Kennedy.

   (d) The Baby Ruth candy bar was actually named after Grover Cleveland's baby daughter, Ruth.

12. Which of the following sentences is correct?

   (a) For example, thousands of edible termites can be raised in a 6-foot mound the same number of cattle requires hundreds of acres of grassland.

   (b) For example, thousands of edible termites can be raised in a 6-foot mound, the same number of cattle requires hundreds of acres of grassland.

   (c) For example, thousands of edible termites can be raised in a 6-foot mound; the same number of cattle requires hundreds of acres of grassland.

   (d) For example, thousands of edible termites can be raised in a 6-foot mound however the same number of cattle requires hundreds of acres of grassland.

13. Which of the following sentences is correct?

   (a) We may think of insects as dirty, they are actually cleaner than other creatures.

   (b) We may think of insects as dirty they are actually cleaner than other creatures.

   (c) We may think of insects as dirty, but they are actually cleaner than other creatures.

   (d) We may think of insects as dirty since they are actually cleaner than other creatures.

14. Which of the following sentences is correct?

   (a) More than one million species of insects and worms exist, and humans can eat about 1,400 of these species.

   (b) More than one million species of insects and worms exist, humans can eat about 1,400 of these species.

   (c) More than one million species of insects and worms exist humans can eat about 1,400 of these species.

   (d) More than one million species of insects and worms exist so humans can eat about 1,400 of these species.

15. Which of the following sentences is correct?

   (a) Those polled were most repulsed about American fast food, they had difficulty with the concept of washing down ground beef with melted ice cream.

   (b) Those polled were most repulsed about American fast food they had difficulty with the concept of washing down ground beef with melted ice cream.

   (c) Those polled were most repulsed about American fast food, they had difficulty with the concept of washing down ground beef with melted ice cream.

   (d) Those polled were most repulsed about American fast food because they had difficulty with the concept of washing down ground beef with melted ice cream.

16. Which of the following sentences is correct?

   (a) You know that insects are healthful, but what do they taste like.

   (b) You know that insects are healthful what do they taste like!

   (c) You know that insects are healthful, what do they taste like?

   (d) You know that insects are healthful, but what do they taste like?

Further Exercises

Correct all the sentence errors in the following paragraph.

   Not surprisingly each type of insects has its own taste. One type of caterpillar has been compared to a mushroom omelet a Mexican stinkbug has a pleasant cinnamon flavor despite its unappealing name. Catherine Fowler a professor of anthropology at the University of Nevada, Reno described the taste of Pandora moth caterpillars as "very good like scrambled egg omelet with mushrooms." Tom Turpin a professor of Entomology at Purdue University enjoys "chocolate chirpy cookies" chocolate chip cookies with roasted crickets. Gene DeFoliart likes greater wax moth larvae, tastes like bacon when deep fried.

ANSWER KEY

True-False Questions

   1. T   2. F   3. T   4. F   5. T   6. T   7. F   8. F   9. F   10. T   11. T   12. T
   13. F   14. F   15. T   16. F   17. T   18. F   19. T   20. T

Completion Questions

1. main   2. comma splice   3. run-on sentences   4. Independent   5. Dependent   6. semicolon   7. nonetheless   8. dependent clause   9. main clause   10. independent   11. can   12. personal style   13. simpler   14. concise   15. cut off from

Multiple-Choice Questions

1. b   2. c   3. c   4. d   5. b   6. b   7. a   8. c   9. d   10. a   11. b   12. c   13. c   14. a   15. d   16. d

Further Exercises

Not surprisingly, each type of insect has its own taste. One type of caterpillar has been compared to a mushroom omelet; a Mexican stinkbug has a pleasant cinnamon flavor despite its unappealing name. Catherine Fowler, a professor of anthropology at the University of Nevada, Reno, described the taste of Pandora moth caterpillars as "very good—like a scrambled egg omelet with mushrooms." Tom Turpin, a professor of entomology at Purdue University, enjoys "chocolate chirpy cookies," which are chocolate chip cookies with roasted crickets. Gene DeFoliart likes greater wax moth larvae, which taste like bacon when deep fried.

CHAPTER 9

Sentence Coordination and Subordination

Y ou should read this chapter if you need to review or learn about

→ Coordinating dependent and independent clauses to create clear and logical sentences

→ Subordinating clauses to make your sentences more concise and graceful

→ Achieving parallel structure in your sentences

Get Started

Here, you'll learn how to decide which parts of your sentences to emphasize by using *coordination* and *subordination*. When you coordinate and subordinate, you establish clear and logical relationships between ideas. You will also learn how to use *parallel structure* by placing ideas in matching (or parallel) forms.

Coordinating Sentence Parts

In Chapter 8, you learned how to connect the parts of a sentence to avoid run-on sentences and sentence fragments. There's more to connecting sentence parts than just linking them, however. You have to decide which parts of each sentence to emphasize and why. The proper emphasis helps you communicate your ideas in writing with strength and style.

Sometimes you want to show that two or more ideas are equally important in a sentence. In such cases, you're looking to *coordinate*. Sentence *coordination* links ideas of equal importance. This process gives your writing balance by bringing together related independent clauses. Coordination involves using the right word or mark of punctuation to show different relationships between ideas.

There are four different ways to coordinate sentence parts:

1. Use a coordinating conjunction.
2. Use a pair of correlative conjunctions.
3. Use a semicolon.
4. Use a semicolon and a conjunctive adverb.

Let's look at each method now.

1. Use a coordinating conjunction.

As you write, use the coordinating conjunction that conveys the precise relationship between ideas that you seek. Each of the coordinating conjunctions has a different meaning, as the following chart shows:

Coordinating Conjunction	Meaning	Function
and	in addition to	to link ideas
but	however	to contrast ideas
for	as a result	to show cause
nor	negative	to reinforce negative
or	choice	to show possibilities
so	therefore	to show result
yet	however	to show contrast or difference

2. Use a pair of correlative conjunctions.
   Link sentences with a correlative conjunction if you want to show a balance between two independent clauses.
   either . . . or   neither . . . nor
   not only . . . but also   both . . . and

3. Use a semicolon.

Link independent clauses with a semicolon to show that the ideas are of equal importance.

A cause is what happens; the effect is the result.

The mechanic adjusted the carburetor; Tina's car now runs smoothly.

4. Use a semicolon and a conjunctive adverb.

As you learned in Chapter 8, there are many different conjunctive adverbs. Some are single words; others are phrases.

consequently	furthermore	therefore
nevertheless	as a result	for example
however	nonetheless	in addition

A semicolon and a conjunctive adverb together indicate different relationships, depending on the conjunctive adverb. The relationships are chiefly examples, continuation, and contrast.

I adore chili; unfortunately, it doesn't adore me!

The invention of air-conditioners has greatly influenced major migration trends; for example, Sunbelt cities such as Phoenix, Atlanta, Dallas, and Houston would never have grown as successfully without air-conditioning.

Follow these steps when you coordinate independent clauses:

- Decide which ideas can and should be combined.
- Select the method of coordination that shows the appropriate relationship between ideas.

Each way to coordinate sentences establishes a slightly different relationship between ideas. Often, there's no "right" answer when you're choosing which conjunctions and punctuation to use to coordinate ideas. As always, keep the "big three" considerations in mind:

- *Audience.* Your readers and their expectations
- *Purpose.* Why you are writing (to entertain, instruct, persuade, describe)
- *Style.* Your personal choices in diction (words) and sentence structure

With practice, you'll discover that some sentences are smoother and more logical than others. Study the following examples:

Uncoordinated: The dog's fur was tangled. We took her in for grooming.

Coordinated: The dog's fur was tangled, so we took her in for grooming.

The dog's fur was tangled; therefore, we took her in for grooming.

The dog's fur was tangled; as a result, we took her in for grooming.

Uncoordinated: There have been many controversial World Series. The most infamous was certainly the thrown World Series of 1919.

Coordinated: There have been many controversial World Series, but the most infamous was certainly the thrown World Series of 1919.

There have been many controversial World Series; however, the most infamous was certainly the thrown World Series of 1919.

Uncoordinated:	Jack lost his briefcase. Jack lost his cell phone.
Coordinated:	Jack lost both his briefcase and his cell phone.

Jack lost not only his briefcase but also his cell phone.

Uncoordinated:	Each year it seems to get harder to pay for a college education. At least $500 million in private-sector money is available to help students pay for their college education.
Coordinated:	Each year it seems to get harder to pay for a college education, but at least $500 million in private-sector money is available to help students pay for their college education.

Each year it seems to get harder to pay for a college education; however, at least $500 million in private-sector money is available to help students pay for their college education.

Quick Tip

Be careful not to connect unrelated ideas, establish a vague connection among ideas, or connect too many ideas in one sentence. These stylistic choices often create confusing sentences.

Subordinating Sentence Parts

Subordination is connecting two unequal but related clauses with a subordinating conjunction to form a complex sentence. *Coordination* shows the relationship among equal independent clauses; *subordination,* in contrast, shows the relationship between ideas of unequal rank.

When you subordinate one part of a sentence to another, you make the dependent clause develop the main clause. Subordination helps you develop your ideas, trace relationships among ideas, and emphasize one idea over the other.

Therefore, you will want to use subordination to give your writing (and speech!) greater logic, coherence, and unity.

As with sentence coordination, sentence subordination calls for logic and thought.

Follow these four steps to subordinate sentence ideas:

1. First choose the idea or clause that you think is the most important.

2. Then make this your main clause by adding a subject or verb, if necessary. Make sure the main clause expresses a complete idea, too.

3. Choose the subordinating conjunction that best expresses the relationship between the main clause and the dependent clause.

4. Decide whether to place the main clause or the dependent clause first. See which order helps you achieve your purpose and appeal to your audience.

There are many subordinating conjunctions, including *after, although, because, before, if, though, since, when, till, unless, wherever, where.* The following chart shows some of the most common subordinating conjunctions and the relationships between ideas that they show.

Subordinating Conjunctions	Relationship
as, because	cause, reason
whether, rather than, than	choice
even if, if, unless, provided that	condition
though, even though, although	contrast
so, so that, in order that, that	effect, result
wherever, where	location
since, until, when, while, after, before, once, whenever	time

With practice, you'll discover that some sentences are smoother and more logical than others. Study the following examples:

Not subordinated: It snowed all night. School was closed the following day.

Subordinated: *Because* it snowed all night, school was closed the following day.

  Since it snowed all night, school was closed the following day.

Not subordinated: About two million dollars had been bet on the Cincinnati Reds to win. The White Sox were favored five to one.

Subordinated: *Even though* the White Sox were favored five to one, about two million dollars had been bet on the Cincinnati Reds to win.

  Although the White Sox were favored five to one, about two million dollars had been bet on the Cincinnati Reds to win.

Not subordinated: A tornado can pick up a house and drop it hundreds of feet away. These are extremely dangerous storms.

Subordinated: *Since* a tornado can pick up a house and drop it hundreds of feet away, these are extremely dangerous storms.

Not subordinated: The case was finally tried. The three men denied having made any confessions. They denied having been involved in any way in the rigging scheme. There was no proof against them.

Subordinated: *When* the case was finally tried, the three men denied having made any confessions. They also denied having been involved in any way in the rigging scheme because there was no proof against them.

When the case was finally tried, the three men denied having made any confessions and having been involved in any way in the rigging scheme because there was no proof against them.

Not subordinated: A tornado is one of the smallest of all types of storms. It is one of the most dangerous of all storms because of its swiftly spinning winds and unpredictable path.

Subordinated: *Even though* a tornado is one of the smallest of all types of storms, it is one of the most dangerous of all storms because of its swiftly spinning winds and unpredictable path.

Be careful not to switch the main clause and the dependent clause when you subordinate. If you put the main idea in a dependent clause, your sentence will not be logical.

Illogical: Because people stared at her, Rikki wore a see-through blouse.

Cause and effect are reversed, so the sentence doesn't make sense.

Logical: Because Rikki wore a see-through blouse, people stared at her.

Coordination versus Subordination

How can you decide which ideas need to be coordinated and which ones need to be subordinated? Base your decision on the ideas in your sentences. As you read in the previous section, rely on the logic of the sentence. Here are some guidelines you can use as you're deciding whether to coordinate or subordinate:

- *Coordinate* when you want to link related independent clauses.
- *Subordinate* when you want to put the most important idea in the main clause.

Here are some examples.

Two clauses: The ground began to tremble. The air was heavy with fear.

Coordinated: The ground began to tremble *and* the air was heavy with fear.

Subordinated: *When* the ground began to tremble, the air was heavy with fear.

subordinate clause   main clause

The emphasis is on the feeling of fear, the information in the main clause.

Subordinated: The air was heavy with fear *as* the ground began to tremble.

main clause   subordinate clause

The emphasis is on trembling ground, the information in the main clause.

Parallel Structure

In 1946, Winston Churchill traveled to Fulton, Missouri, *to deliver* a speech and *to be present* at the dedication of a bust in his honor. After his speech, an *attractive* and *ample* woman approached the wartime prime minister of England and said, "Mr. Churchill, *I have traveled* over a hundred miles for the unveiling of your bust." Churchill, who was known *far* and *wide* for his quick wit, responded, "I assure you, in that regard, *I would gladly return the favor.*"

Parallel structure means putting ideas of the same rank in the same grammatical structure. In the above anecdote, the italicized words and phrases show parallel structure. Your writing and speech should have parallel words, phrases, and clauses. Parallel structure gives your writing many admirable strengths, including tempo, stress, balance, and conciseness.

1. *Parallel words* share the same part of speech (such as nouns, adjectives, or verbs) and tense (if the words are verbs).

   To some people, traveling by air is *safe, inexpensive,* and *convenient.*

   To others, it's *dangerous, expensive,* and *inconvenient.*

   You should eat foods that are *nourishing* as well as *tasty.*

2. *Parallel phrases* contain modifiers.

   Polyester shirts wash easily, drip-dry quickly, and wear durably.

   Nick took the new job to learn more about finance, make important connections, and get a health plan.

   "For taking away our Charters, abolishing our laws, and altering the Forms of our Government . . ." (Declaration of Independence)

3. *Parallel clauses* can be complete sentences or dependent clauses.

   I came, I saw, I conquered.

   "Our chiefs are killed; Looking-Glass is dead; Ta-Hool-Shute is dead." (Chief Joseph's surrender speech, 1877)

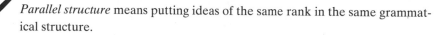 Sentence *coordination* links ideas of equal importance.

Sentence *subordination* connects two unequal but related clauses with a subordinating conjunction to form a complex sentence.

Parallel structure means putting ideas of the same rank in the same grammatical structure.

QUESTIONS

True-False Questions

1. Sentence *coordination* links ideas of equal importance.

2. Each of the coordinating conjunctions has a different meaning.

3. *Subordination* involves using the right word or mark of punctuation to show different relationships between ideas.

4. Correlative conjunctions always come in pairs, such as "either . . . or" and "not only . . . but also."

5. Link sentences with a subordinating conjunction if you want to show a balance between two independent clauses.

6. Link independent clauses with a semicolon to show that the information in the main clause is not as important as the information in the subordinate clause.

7. Each way to coordinate sentences establishes a slightly different relationship between ideas.

8. There is always a clearly "right" conjunction and punctuation to use when you coordinate ideas.

9. *Coordination* shows the relationship among equal independent clauses; *subordination*, in contrast, shows the relationship between ideas of unequal rank.

10. When you coordinate one part of a sentence to another, you make the dependent clause develop the main clause.

11. If you put the main idea in a dependent clause, your sentence will not be logical.

12. *Subordinate* when you want to link related independent clauses.

13. *Coordinate* when you want to put the most important idea in the main clause.

14. *Parallel words* share the same part of speech (such as nouns, adjectives, or verbs) and tense (if the words are verbs).

15. The following sentence has parallel adjectives:

Egypt, a long, narrow, fertile strip of land in northeastern Africa, is the only place in the world where pyramids were built.

Completion Questions

Select the word that best completes each sentence.

1. A lightning bolt lasts a fraction of a second, (so, but) it has enough power—30 million volts—to light up all of Miami.

2. (And, Because) the average thunderstorm is more powerful than an atomic bomb, injuries from these storms are not uncommon.

3. All the following are coordinating conjunctions except *for, but, or* (*since, and*).

4. All the following are subordinating conjunctions except *since, because, although* (*when, nor*).

5. All the following are conjunctive adverbs except *consequently, furthermore, therefore,* (*nevertheless, and*).

6. (*Coordination, Subordination*) is connecting two unequal but related clauses with a subordinating conjunction to form a complex sentence.

7. (*Subordination, Parallel structure*) means putting ideas of the same rank in the same grammatical structure.

8. The film industry changed from silent films to the "talkies" in the late 1920s, (when, after) the success in 1927 of *The Jazz Singer.*

9. Ari is very good about staying in shape: He likes to ride his bicycle, to jog around the track, and (swimming, to go swimming).

10. The committee considered the letter, talked about its major points, and (the unanimous decision was made to ignore it, unanimously decided to ignore it).

Multiple-Choice Questions

Choose the best answer to each question.

1. You can coordinate independent clauses by using all the following methods *except*
    (a) Coordinating conjunctions
    (b) Correlative conjunctions
    (c) A semicolon and a conjunctive adverb
    (d) Subordinating conjunctions

2. When you coordinate independent clauses, you should decide which ideas can and should be combined and then
    (a) Select the method of coordination that shows the appropriate relationship between ideas.
    (b) Use the subordinating conjunction that most clearly expresses your ideas.
    (c) Add a semicolon to link ideas.
    (d) String together as many ideas as you can.

3. When you decide how to coordinate or subordinate ideas, you should always consider your
    (a) Audience
    (b) Purpose
    (c) Handwriting
    (d) Style

4. Which revision best combines ideas?
   Ancient Egypt had an abundance of rocks quarried close to the banks of the Nile. These rocks had to be brought from quarries to the building sites.
    (a) Ancient Egypt had an abundance of rocks quarried close to the banks of the Nile, so these rocks had to be brought from quarries to the building sites.
    (b) Ancient Egypt had an abundance of rocks quarried close to the banks of the Nile, when these rocks had to be brought from quarries to the building sites.
    (c) Ancient Egypt had an abundance of rocks quarried close to the banks of the Nile, but these rocks had to be brought from quarries to the building sites.
    (d) Since ancient Egypt had an abundance of rocks quarried close to the banks of the Nile; these rocks had to be brought from quarries to the building sites.

5. Which revision best combines ideas?

   Darrow invented a board game he called "Monopoly." Monopoly made him a millionaire. This did not happen at first.

   (a) This did not happen at first, but Darrow invented a board game he called "Monopoly." When Monopoly made him a millionaire.

   (b) Darrow invented a board game he called "Monopoly," which made him a millionaire, although not at first.

   (c) Because Darrow invented a board game he called "Monopoly," Monopoly made him a millionaire. This did not happen at first.

   (d) Although Monopoly made him a millionaire, Darrow invented a board game he called "Monopoly," but this did not happen at first.

6. Which revision best combines ideas?

   Parker Brothers turned the game down. They felt it was too complicated to play.

   (a) Parker Brothers turned the game down and they felt it was too complicated to play.

   (b) Since Parker Brothers turned the game down, they felt it was too complicated to play.

   (c) When Parker Brothers turned the game down, they felt it was too complicated to play.

   (d) Parker Brothers turned the game down because they felt it was too complicated to play.

7. Which revision best combines ideas?

   Large numbers of people began flooding into southern Florida more than a century ago. The amount of water that once flowed south through the Everglades has been drastically reduced.

   (a) Ever since large numbers of people began flooding into southern Florida more than a century ago, the amount of water that once flowed south through the Everglades has been drastically reduced.

   (b) Large numbers of people began flooding into southern Florida more than a century ago, but the amount of water that once flowed south through the Everglades has been drastically reduced.

   (c) Large numbers of people began flooding into southern Florida more than a century ago, yet the amount of water that once flowed south through the Everglades has been drastically reduced.

   (d) When the amount of water that once flowed south through the Everglades has been drastically reduced, large numbers of people began flooding into southern Florida more than a century ago.

8. Which choice best connects the following sentence?

   It took almost a year for three men to sign confessions admitting the series had been fixed. The men were Lefty Williams, Eddie Cicotte, and J. Jackson. The men admitted they were in on the scam.

   (a) It took almost a year for three men—Lefty Williams, Eddie Cicotte, and J. Jackson—to sign confessions admitting the series had been fixed and they were in on it.

(b) Lefty Williams, Eddie Cicotte, and J. Jackson admitted they were in on the scam when it took almost a year for them to sign confessions admitting the series had been fixed.

(c) Since it took almost a year for Lefty Williams, Eddie Cicotte, and J. Jackson to sign confessions admitting the series had been fixed, they admitted they were in on the scam.

(d) It took almost a year for Lefty Williams, Eddie Cicotte, and J. Jackson to sign confessions admitting the series had been fixed; however, the men admitted they were in on the scam.

9. Which revision best combines ideas?

The water declined. The freshwater bird population has declined more than 90 percent since the early 1900s.

(a) The freshwater bird population has declined more than 90 percent since the early 1900s and the water declined.

(b) The water declined because the freshwater bird population has declined more than 90 percent since the early 1900s.

(c) The water declined, but the freshwater bird population has declined more than 90 percent since the early 1900s.

(d) As a result of the declining water, the freshwater bird population has declined more than 90 percent since the early 1900s.

10. Which revision best combines ideas?

There are still ample physical reminders of the history of the Native Americans in Florida. Impressive burial mounds, dating back hundreds of years, can be found along many of the rivers, for instance.

(a) Impressive burial mounds, dating back hundreds of years, can be found along many of the rivers, for instance; there are still ample physical reminders of the history of the Native Americans in Florida.

(b) Since there are still ample physical reminders of the history of the Native Americans in Florida, impressive burial mounds, dating back hundreds of years, can be found along many of the rivers, for instance.

(c) Although impressive burial mounds, dating back hundreds of years, can be found along many of the rivers, for instance, there are still ample physical reminders of the history of the Native Americans in Florida.

(d) There are still ample physical reminders of the history of the Native Americans in Florida; impressive burial mounds, dating back hundreds of years, can be found along many of the rivers, for instance.

Further Exercises

Recombine the sentences in the following paragraphs to create a more logical and graceful style.

1. Lightning often strike twice in the same place. It is more likely to do so. Why is this so? Lightning is an electric current. As with all electric currents or discharges, lightning will follow the path of least resistance. It will take the route that is easiest for it to travel on.

Air is a very poor conductor of electricity. Almost anything else that helps to bridge the gap between the ground and a cloud will offer a more convenient path and thus "attract" the lightning. This includes a high tree, a building (especially one with a metal framework), a tall hill.

2. In 1866, John Styth Pemberton came up with a headache medicine he called "Coca-Cola." He had taken the wine out of the French Wine Coca. He added some caffeine. The medicine tasted so terrible that at the last minute he added some extract of kola nut. He added a few other oils. He sold it to soda fountains in used bottles. A few weeks later, a man with a terrible headache hauled himself into a drugstore. The man asked for a spoonful of Coca-Cola. The druggist was too lazy to stir the headache remedy into a glass of water. He mixed the syrup in some seltzer water. The seltzer water was closer to where he was standing. The customer liked the carbonated version better than the uncarbonated one. Other customers agreed. From then on, Coca-Cola was served as a carbonated drink.

3. Some time near the beginning of the seventh century, a monk formed some leftover dough into a looped twist. Some sources claim that the twists were meant to represent the folded arms of children at prayer, but even by a considerable stretch of the imagination it is hard to match a pretzel's shape with the usual position of arms at prayer. The pretzels soon became popular and were often given to children who were faithful in their religious observations. As a result, the baked and salted dough came to be called *pretiola,* the Latin for "little reward." From *pretiola* to *pretzel* is only a small step.

ANSWER KEY

True-False Questions

1. T   2. T   3. F   4. T   5. F   6. F   7. T   8. F   9. T   10. F   11. T   12. F
13. F   14. T   15. T

Completion Questions

1. but   2. Because   3. since   4. nor   5. and   6. Subordinating
7. Parallel structure   8. after   9. to go swimming   10. Unanimously decided
to ignore it

Multiple-Choice Questions

1. d   2. a   3. c   4. c   5. b   6. d   7. a   8. a   9. d   10. d

Further Exercises

Answers will vary; here are some sample answers.

1. Not only does lightning often strike twice in the same place, but it is also more likely to do so. Why is this so? Lightning is an electric current. As with all electric currents or discharges, lightning will follow the path of least resistance, so it will take the route that is

easiest for it to travel on. Since air is a very poor conductor of electricity, almost anything else that helps to bridge the gap between the ground and a cloud—a high tree, a building (especially one with a metal framework), a tall hill—will offer a more convenient path and thus "attract" the lightning.

2. In 1866, John Styth Pemberton came up with a headache medicine he called "Coca-Cola." He had taken the wine out of the French Wine Coca and added some caffeine, but the medicine tasted so terrible that at the last minute he added some extract of kola nut and a few other oils. He sold it to soda fountains in used bottles. A few weeks later, a man with a terrible headache hauled himself into a drugstore and asked for a spoonful of Coca-Cola. The druggist was too lazy to stir the headache remedy into a glass of water, so he mixed the syrup in some seltzer water because it was closer to where he was standing. The customer liked the carbonated version better than the uncarbonated one; other customers agreed. From then on, Coca-Cola was served as a carbonated drink.

3. Some time near the beginning of the seventh century, a monk formed some leftover dough into a looped twist. Some sources claim that the twists were meant to represent the folded arms of children at prayer. Even by a considerable stretch of the imagination it is hard to match a pretzel's shape with the usual position of arms at prayer. The pretzels soon became popular. The pretzels were often given to children who were faithful in their religious observations. As a result, the baked and salted dough came to be called *pretiola*, the Latin for "little reward." From *pretiola* to *pretzel* is only a small step.

PART 4

A Writer's Tools

CHAPTER 10

Punctuation

Y ou should read this chapter if you need to review or learn about

Do I Need to Read This Chapter?

→ Apostrophes, brackets, colons

→ Commas, dashes, ellipsis

→ Exclamation marks, hyphens

→ Parentheses, periods, question marks, quotation marks

→ Semicolons, slashes

Get Started

Using the correct punctuation helps you convey your ideas exactly as you intend them. In this chapter, you'll review the basic rules of punctuation. This will help you express yourself clearly in writing. The punctuation marks are arranged in alphabetical order for ease of use.

Apostrophes

The apostrophe (') is used in three ways:

1. To show possession (ownership)
2. To show plural forms
3. To show where a letter or number has been omitted

Let's examine each guideline in depth.

1. Use an apostrophe to show possession.

- With singular nouns or pronouns *not* ending in *s*, add an apostrophe and an *s*.

  a rocket   a rocket's red glare

  a flag   a flag's stripes

  someone   someone's wish

  anyone   anyone's game

- With singular nouns ending in *s*, add an apostrophe and an *s*.

  James   James's car

  waitress   waitress's suggestion

- If the new word is hard to say, leave off the *s*.

  James' car   waitresses' suggestion

- With plural nouns *not* ending in *s*, add an apostrophe and an *s*.

  men   men's shoes

  people   people's feelings

- With plural nouns ending in *s*, add an apostrophe after the *s*.

  several computers   several computers' hard drives

  three teachers   three teachers' lesson plans

If you are having difficulty deciding where to put the apostrophe and whether to add an *s*, try following these two steps:

- To figure out if ownership is involved, ask yourself: "To whom does it belong?"
- If the answer is a singular noun or pronoun, follow that rule. If it's a plural noun, follow that rule.

  You have the phrase "my friends party."

  Ask: To whom does the party belong?

  Answer: It belongs to my friend. *Friend* is singular. Therefore, the phrase reads: "My friend's party."

2. Use an apostrophe to show plural forms.

- Use an apostrophe and *s* to show the plural of a number, symbol, or letter, or words used to name themselves.

  three 7's

  two ?'s

  your *u*'s look like *w*'s

  There are too many distracting *like's* and *um's* in her speech.

3. Use an apostrophe to show where a letter or number has been omitted.

- Use an apostrophe to show where letters have been left out of contractions. Recall that *contractions* are two words combined. When you contract words, add an apostrophe in the space where the letters have been taken out.

  can not   can't

  I will   I'll

- Use an apostrophe to show numbers have been left out of a date.

  the '70s   the '90s

Quick Tip

Don't confuse contractions with possessive pronouns. Study the following chart:

Contraction	Possessive Pronoun
it's (it is)	its
you're (you are)	your
they're (they are)	their
who's (who is)	whose

Brackets

Brackets are [ ]. Do not confuse them with parentheses, which are curved like this (). Brackets have only two very narrowly defined uses.

1. Use brackets for editorial clarification.

   Children's author Jackie Ogburn puts it this way: "It's not that 'message' isn't a part of the work. It's just that it's usually the least *interesting* part [emphasis hers]."

2. Use brackets to enclose words that you insert in a quotation.

When you integrate quoted words into a text, you may have to change a few words to fit the structure of your sentences. Enclose any changes you make in brackets.

Original quote: "This pedagogical approach reduces all our work to the literary equivalent of vitamins." (Ogburn 305)

Quotation with brackets: The primary reason the people involved in creating children's books detest this attitude so much is that "[it] reduces all our work to the literary equivalent of vitamins." (Ogburn 305)

Colons

1. Use a colon after an independent clause to introduce a list. Remember that an independent clause is a complete sentence.

The colon is two dots, one on top of each other, like this (:).

If you really want to lose weight, you must give up the following sweets: cake, pie, candy, and cookies.

2. Use a colon after an independent clause to introduce a quotation.

Robert Lawson speaks impatiently of the good intentions that direct the current trends in children's books: "Some of this scattered band may be educators or psychologists or critics, but they are all animated by a ruthless determination to do children good through their books; it is these people who start the theories and fads that are the bane of authors and illustrators and editors and a pain in the neck to children." (Fenner, 47)

Quick Tip

Place colons *outside* closing quotation marks.

3. Use a colon before the part of a sentence that explains what has just been stated.

Our store has a fixed policy: We will not be undersold.

4. Use a colon after the salutation of a business letter.

Dear Dr. Lewis:

To Whom It May Concern:

5. Use a colon to distinguish chapter from verse in a Biblical citation, hours from minutes, and titles from subtitles.

Song of Songs 4:15

10:15 A.M.

Eating Healthy: A Complete Guide

Commas

Commas are the most frequently used marks of punctuation in English. In fact, commas occur in writing twice as often as all other marks of punctuation combined!

Commas tell us how to read and understand sentences, because they tell us where to pause. A correctly placed comma helps move readers from the beginning of a sentence to the end.

Here's the overall comma alert:

As you write, don't add commas just because you paused in your reading. Since every-one pauses at different times, a pause isn't a reliable way to judge comma use. Instead, rely on the rules that govern comma use.

And here are those guidelines:

1. Use a comma to set off parts of a sentence.

   - Use a comma to separate parts of a compound sentence. Use the comma before the coordinating conjunction.

     The movie was sold out, *so* we decided to have an early dinner.

     The movie was a blockbuster, *but* we arrived early enough to get seats.

     Our friends are easy-going, *and* they don't get upset when plans change.

   - Use a comma to set off dialogue.

     Martha said, "This movie won an Academy Award."

     "This movie," Martha said, "won an Academy Award."

     "This movie won an Academy Award," Martha said.

   - Use a comma to separate the parts of an address. Do not use a comma before the zip code in an address.

     Rick lives at 163 East Plains Drive, Boston, MA 89012

2. Use a comma after introductory and concluding expressions.

   - Use a comma after an introductory word.

     Yes, I will be coming to the retirement party.

     However, I won't be able to bring a macaroni salad.

   - Use a comma after an introductory phrase.

     To get a good night's sleep, you should practice relaxation techniques.

     Beginning tomorrow, the store will be open until midnight.

   - Use a comma after an introductory clause.

     Although the sky is overcast, I don't think that it will rain this afternoon.

     Since you can't do the dishes, could you please walk the dog tonight?

   - Use a comma after the greeting of an informal letter.

     Dear Mom,   Dear Mickey,

   - Use a comma at the close of any letter.

     Yours truly,   Sincerely,

Quick Tip

Remember: The coordinating conjunctions are *and, but, for, or, nor, so, yet.*

3. Use a comma after interrupting words and expressions.

- Use a comma to set off interrupting words and expressions.

    The State University of New York, *did you know,* has 64 campuses scattered across New York State.

- Use a comma to set off words of direct address (words that tell to whom a remark is addressed).

    Nanci, please clean up your room.

    Please clean up your room, Nanci.

- Use a comma with names and titles.

    Ms. Barbara Gilson, Editorial Director

    Laurie Rozakis, Ph.D.

- Use a comma to set off words in *apposition* (words that give additional information about the preceding or following word or expression).

    A good eater, my baby will be off the bottle soon.

    My baby, a good eater, will be off the bottle soon.

 • Use a comma to set off a *nonessential clause* (a clause that can be omitted without changing the sentence's basic meaning).

    Elizabeth II, who was born in 1926 in London, is the queen of England.

    Prince Charles, Elizabeth's first child, was born in 1948.

- Use a comma to separate items in a series. The comma before *and* in a series of items is optional.

    The store had a sale on hot dogs, watermelon, and paper plates.

Quick Tip

Never use commas to set off an *essential clause,* a clause that cannot be omitted. Some states retest drivers *who are over age 65* to check their ability to drive safely.

---

4. Use commas to prevent misreading.

- Use a comma to clarify any potentially confusing sentences.

Confusing:	Those who can practice many hours every day.
Clear:	Those who can, practice many hours every day.
Rewritten:	Those who can practice, do so many hours every day.

Confusing:	Luisa dressed and sang for an enthusiastic crowd.
Clear:	Luisa dressed, and sang for an enthusiastic crowd.
Rewritten:	After Luisa dressed, she sang for an enthusiastic crowd.

Of course, as the rewritten examples show, you're usually much better off revising the sentences so there is no possibility of your audience misreading your words.

5. Use commas with numbers. Do not use commas when writing telephone numbers, page numbers, or years.

- Use a comma between the day of the month and the year.

    December 7, 1941   July 20, 1969

- Use commas to show thousands, millions, and so on.

    5,000   50,000   500,000   5,000,000

Dashes

A dash (—) is *not* the same as a hyphen. The dash, or a pair of dashes, lets you interrupt a sentence to add emphasis with additional information. Use dashes lightly or you risk creating a breathless, overly informal style.

Use a dash to emphasize an example, a definition, or a contrast.

Two of the strongest animals in the jungle—the elephant and gorilla—are vegetarians.

Two of the strongest animals in the jungle are vegetarians—the elephant and gorilla.

Ellipsis

The ellipsis (three spaced dots) is used to show that you have left something out of a passage you are quoting. You can also use ellipsis to show a pause in a conversation.

1. Use the ellipsis to show that you have deleted words or sentences from a passage you are quoting.

    Abraham Lincoln said: "Four score and seven years ago our fathers brought forth . . . a new nation, conceived in liberty and dedicated to the proposition that all men are created equal."

2. Use the ellipsis to show a pause or interruption.

    "No," I said. "I . . . I need some time to think about your offer."

Quick Tip

Don't use the ellipsis to show that words have been omitted from the beginning of a sentence. Just omit the words and begin the quote.

Exclamation Marks

Use an exclamation mark after an exclamatory sentence.

How dare you say that to me!

You can't possibly go out wearing that dress!

Hyphens

A *hyphen* (-) is smaller than a dash. Use a hyphen to show a break in words. Traditionally, a hyphen was used to show a word break at the end of a line. However, modern computer software has virtually eliminated this use of the hyphen.

1. Use a hyphen in certain compound nouns.

    pint-sized great-grandmother

2. Use hyphens in written-out fractions and in written-out compound numbers from twenty-one to ninety-nine.

    one-half   fifty-five

Parentheses

Use parentheses to set off nonessential information. In essence, the information in the parentheses is a nonessential modifier because it gives the reader additional information that is not crucial.

1. Use parentheses to enclose additional information in a sentence.

    Capitalize all proper nouns and proper adjectives (see Chapter 11).

2. Use parentheses to enclose numbers or letters.

    To prepare spaghetti, follow these steps in order: (1) Bring a pot of lightly salted water to boil; (2) add pasta; (3) cook about 10 minutes, to taste.

Periods

1. Use a period after a complete sentence.

   The shrimp's heart is in its head.

   In the Arctic, the sun sometimes appears to be square.

2. Use a period after most abbreviations and initials. If an abbreviation comes at the end of a sentence, do not add another period.

   Dr.   Ms.   Jr.   John F. Kennedy

3. Don't use a period after acronyms.

   CNN   ABC   CBS

4. Use a period after each Roman numeral, letter, or number in an outline.

   I.
     A.
     B.
       1.
       2.

Question Marks

Use a question mark after a question.

Where is the complaint desk?

Will the store be open late tonight?

Quotation Marks

1. Use quotation marks to set off a speaker's exact words.

   "Did you eat the entire bag of chips?" Debbie squealed.

2. Use quotation marks to set off the titles of short works such as poems, essays, songs, short stories, and magazine articles.

   "The Lottery" by Shirley Jackson (short story)

   "Self-Reliance" by Ralph Waldo Emerson (essay)

   "We've Only Just Begun" by the Carpenters (song)

3. Use single quotation marks to set off quoted material or the titles of short works within a quotation enclosed by double quotation marks.

   "Did you read 'The Ransom of Red Chief' last night?" the teacher asked.

4. Use quotation marks to set off words used for emphasis or a definition.

The proposed "tax reform" is really nonsense.

Semicolons

A semicolon is a comma and period combined, like this (;). The semicolon's structure shows you that the semicolon is a hybrid of a comma and a period. It's a stronger stop than a comma but not as strong as a period.

1. Use a semicolon between closely related independent clauses when the coordinating conjunction has been left out.

The chef cooked far too much chicken; we eagerly devoured the excess.

2. Use a semicolon between main clauses connected by conjunctive adverbs such as *however, nevertheless, moreover, for example,* and *consequently.*

Sarah wanted to be a doctor; however, she faints at the sight of blood.

3. Use a semicolon to join independent clauses when one or both clauses contain a comma.

Glenn, who is an accomplished musician, wanted to perform at his sister's wedding; but he quickly discovered that Marcia, the maid of honor, had other plans for the entertainment.

Slashes

This is a slash (/).

1. Use slashes to separate lines of poetry. Leave a space before and after the slash to show when the line of poetry ends.

As written:

> The band, as fairy legends say,
>
> Was wove on that creating day,
>
> When He, who called with thought to birth
>
> Yon tented sky, this laughing earth.

In running text:

The band, as fairy legends say, / Was wove on that creating day, / When He, who called with thought to birth / Yon tented sky, this laughing earth.

2. Use slashes to show choice.

Devon broke the on/off switch on the toaster.

3. Use slashes in numerical fractions or formulas.

1/2   3/4

It's a Wrap

✔ Punctuation helps readers identify clusters of words between and within sentences.

✔ Between sentences, the most common mark of punctuation is the period; within sentences, the most common mark is the comma.

✔ Hyphens separate word parts; dashes separate sentence parts or sentences.

✔ Semicolons separate complete sentences; colons show lists.

QUESTIONS

True-False Questions

1. With singular nouns or pronouns *not* ending in s, add an apostrophe and an s.

2. With singular nouns ending in s, add an apostrophe but not another s.

3. With plural nouns ending in s, add an apostrophe before the s, as in "Charle's" or "Jame's."

4. With plural nouns *not* ending in s, add an apostrophe and an s, as in "men's suits."

5. Use a comma rather than an apostrophe to show plural forms.

6. Contractions and possessive pronouns are the same, as in "it's/its" "you're/your," and "they're/their."

7. Use a colon after the salutation (greeting) of a business letter.

8. As you write, don't add commas just because you paused in your reading.

9. The following sentence is punctuated correctly:
   We enjoy taking cruises on luxurious ships, but cruises can be costly vacations.

10. Use a comma to separate the parts of an address; be sure use to use a comma before the zip code in an address.

11. Use a comma after an introductory word, phrase, or clause.

12. Use a comma to set off words in *apposition* (words that give additional information about the preceding or following word or expression).

13. Use a comma to set off an *essential clause* (a clause that cannot be omitted without changing the sentence's basic meaning).

14. The ellipsis (three spaced dots) is used to show that you have left something out of a passage you are quoting.

15. Use a period after most abbreviations and initials. If an abbreviation comes at the end of a sentence, be sure to add another period.

Completion Questions

Select the word that best completes each sentence.

1. A (dash, hyphen) is longer than a (dash, hyphen).
2. (Parentheses, Brackets) are curved.
3. Use an apostrophe to show where a letter or number has been omitted in a (contraction, quotation).
4. Use brackets for (showing possession, editorial clarification) and to enclose words you insert in a quotation.
5. The colon is (a dot and a comma, two dots), one symbol on top of the other.
6. Use a colon after an independent clause to introduce a list and a (quotation, question).
7. Use a (semicolon, colon) before part of a sentence that explains what has just been stated.
8. (Periods, Commas) are the most frequently used marks of punctuation in English. In fact, they occur in writing twice as often as all other marks of punctuation combined!
9. Use a comma to separate parts of a compound sentence. Use the comma (after, before) the coordinating conjunction.
10. Use a comma after the greeting of (a business, an informal) letter.
11. Use a (comma, period) after most abbreviations and initials.
12. Use quotation marks to set off a speaker's (paraphrased words, exact words).
13. Use a semicolon between closely related (dependent, independent) clauses when the coordinating conjunction has been left out.
14. Use a semicolon to join independent clauses when one or both clauses contain a (period, comma).
15. Use (commas, slashes) to separate lines of poetry in running text.

Multiple-Choice Questions

Choose the best answer to each question.

1. The apostrophe (') is used in all of the following ways *except*
    (a) To show possession (ownership)
    (b) To show plural forms
    (c) To show where a letter or number has been omitted
    (d) To show where information has been omitted
2. Use a comma in all the following situations *except*
    (a) To separate independent clauses (sentences)
    (b) The close of any letter, business as well as personal
    (c) After interrupting words and expressions
    (d) To set off words of direct address

3. Why is there a comma in the following sentence?
   Those who can, practice many hours every day.
   (a) To set off a nonessential clause
   (b) To prevent misreading
   (c) To show an appositive
   (d) To separate items in a series

4. What mark of punctuation is used to show that you have left something out of a passage you are quoting?
   (a) Brackets
   (b) Parenthesis
   (c) Ellipsis
   (d) Quotation marks

5. Use a dash for all the following reasons *except*
   (a) To emphasize an example
   (b) To show a contrast
   (c) To set off a speaker's direct words
   (d) To set off a definition

6. What mark of punctuation is used to show a break in words?
   (a) Dash
   (b) Slash
   (c) Hyphen
   (d) Colon

7. Use quotation marks to set off the titles of all the following literary works *except*
   (a) Novels
   (b) Poems
   (c) Songs
   (d) Short stories

8. Which sentence is correctly punctuated?
   (a) Tsunamis or seismic sea waves, are gravity waves set in motion by underwater disturbances associated with earthquakes.
   (b) Near its origin, the first wave of a tsunami may be the largest; at greater distances, the largest is normally between the second and seventh wave.
   (c) Tsunamis consist of a decaying train of waves and, may be detectable on tide gauges, for as long as a week.
   (d) These waves are frequently called tidal waves although, they have nothing to do with the tides.

9. Which sentence is correctly punctuated?
   (a) Most natural hazards; can be detected before their threat matures.
   (b) But seisms have no known precursors, so they come without warning.

   (c) For this reason they continue to kill in some areas at a level usually reserved
        for wars and epidemics—the 11,000 dead in northeastern Iran died on
        August 31 1968 not in the ancient past.

   (d) The homeless living are left to cope with fire looting pestilence fear, and the
        burden of rebuilding what the planet so easily shrugs away.

10. Which sentence is correctly punctuated?

   (a) Given by the people of France to the people of the United States as a symbol
        of a shared love of freedom and everlasting friendship, the Statue of Liberty
        is the largest freestanding sculpture ever created.

   (b) It weighs 450000 pounds and rises 1,51 feet above its pedestal.

   (c) More than 100 feet, around, Ms. Liberty boasts eyes two and a half feet wide.

   (d) Her upraised right arm; extends forty two feet.

Further Exercises

Correctly punctuate the following paragraphs:

1. Long-time Boston resident's still talk about the molasses flood that engulfed the citys'
   north end, on January 15 1919 Many people were sitting near the Purity, Distilling Cor-
   porations fifty foot high molasses tank enjoying the unseasonably warm day. The tank was
   filled with over two million gallons of molasses and it was about to burst apart. First
   molasses oozed through, the tanks rivets then the metal bolts popped out the seams burst
   and tons of molasses' burst out in a surge of deadly goo. The first wave over twenty five
   feet high smashed: building's trees people and animals like toys. Sharp pieces of the tank
   sliced through the air injuring scores of people. After the initial destruction molasses, continued to clog the street's for days. Many survivors had to have their clothing cut off dried
   molasses turned clothing into cement. People, were stuck to sidewalks and benches
   molasses glued telephone receiver's to ears and hands. The disaster left over 20 people
   dead and, more than 50 hurt.

2. In many Native American tribes the "shaman" or medicine man acted as a ceremonial
   priest. In other tribe's however the medicine mans job was to treat any one of his people
   who became ill. In his role as a healer the medicine man carried a bag of secret herb's and
   charms to rid the patient of his sickness. Among the tools of his trade were dried finger's
   deer tails drums' rattles' and tiny sacks of herbs. Different tribes used different herbs;
   depending on what was available in the area and through trading. The Dakotas for example relieved asthma with the powdered root of skunk cabbage the Kiowas' stopped dandruff with the soaproot plant.

ANSWER KEY

True-False Questions

   1. T   2. F   3. F   4. T   5. F   6. F   7. T   8. T   9. T   10. F   11. T   12. T
   13. F   14. T   15. F

Completion Questions

1. dash, hyphen   2. Parentheses   3. contraction   4. editorial clarification
5. two dots   6. quotation   7. colon   8. Commas   9. before   10. an informal
11. period   12. exact words   13. independent   14. comma   15. slashes

Multiple-Choice Questions

1. d   2. a   3. b   4. c   5. c   6. c   7. a   8. b   9. b   10. a

Further Exercises

1. Long-time Boston residents still talk about the molasses flood that engulfed the city's north end on January 15, 1919. Many people were sitting near the Purity Distilling Corporation's fifty foot high molasses tank enjoying the unseasonably warm day. The tank was filled with more than two million gallons of molasses—and it was about to burst apart. First, molasses oozed through the tank's rivets. Then the metal bolts popped out, the seams burst, and tons of molasses burst out in a surge of deadly goo. The first wave, over twenty-five feet high, smashed buildings, trees, people and animals like toys. Sharp pieces of the tank sliced through the air, injuring scores of people. After the initial destruction, molasses continued to clog the streets for days. Many survivors had to have their clothing cut off: dried molasses turned clothing into cement. People were stuck to sidewalks and benches; molasses glued telephone receivers to ears and hands. The disaster left more than 20 people dead and more than 50 hurt.

2. In many Native American tribes, the "shaman" or medicine man, acted as a ceremonial priest. In other tribes, however, the medicine man's job was to treat any one of his people who became ill. In his role as a healer, the medicine man carried a bag of secret herbs and charms to rid the patient of his sickness. Among the tools of his trade were dried fingers, deer tails, drums, rattles, and tiny sacks of herbs. Different tribes used different herbs, depending on what was available in the area and through trading. The Dakotas, for example, relieved asthma with the powdered root of skunk cabbage; the Kiowas stopped dandruff with the soaproot plant.

CHAPTER 11

Capitalization and Abbreviations

You should read this chapter if you need to review or learn about

Do I Need
to Read
This Chapter?

➡ The rules governing capitalization

➡ The guidelines for using abbreviations

➡ The "mechanics" of written English

Get Started

Our system of capital and lowercase letters allows writers to point out specific words within a sentence and to signal the start of a new sentence. The rules may seem arbitrary, but you'll soon discover that they function much as traffic signals to help travelers negotiate the highways of written language. This chapter explains the rules that govern the accepted use of capital letters and abbreviations.

Avoiding Capital Offenses: The Rules of Capitalization

Basically, capitalization falls into two categories:

- *Capitalize all proper nouns.* These include names, geographical places, specific historical events, eras, and documents, languages, nationalities, countries, and races.
- *Capitalize the first word at the beginning of a sentence.*

In everyday writing, the rules are clear-cut. However, if you are writing within a specific organization or company, capitalization is mostly a matter of editorial style. The important goal is always the same: Use capital letters consistently within a particular document.

Quick Tip

Today, professional writers and editors tend to use fewer capital letters than was the habit in the past. In the nineteenth century and before, many more nouns were capitalized, as novels from this period reveal.

Let's look at these rules in detail. The proper nouns are divided into separate categories for ease of reference, starting with names and titles.

Capitalize Names and Titles

1. Capitalize each part of a person's name.

   George W. Bush   Jennifer Aniston

   Soupy Sales   Hillary Clinton

   - If a name begins with *d', de, du,* or *von,* capitalize the prefix unless it is preceded by a first name or a title.

Without a first name	Du Pont	Von Karman
With a first name	E. I. du Pont	Theodore von Karman

   - If a name begins with *Mc, O',* or *St.,* capitalize the next letter as well.

     McMannus   O'Neill   St. Claire

   - If the name begins with *la* or *le,* the capitalization varies: *le Blanc* and *Le Blanc* are both correct, for example.

- Capitalize the names of specific animals.

     Rin Tin Tin   Lassie   Morris the cat

- A personal name that is used as a common noun is no longer capitalized. These words are often used in science.

     curie   watt   newton   kelvin

2. Capitalize titles used before a person's name.

President Bush	Chief Scientist Smithson
Dr. Frankenstein	Ms. Brownmiller
Mr. Williams	Professor Chin

For a democracy, we have a surprising number of titles. Here are some of the most common ones:

Religious titles:	Bishop	Reverend
	Father	Sister
	Rabbi	Monsigneur
Military titles	Admiral	Colonel
	Major	Sergeant
	Lieutenant	General
Elected officials:	Mayor	Governor
	President	Senator
	Congressman	Congresswoman
	Secretary	Ambassador
Earned titles:	Doctor	Professor
	Provost	Dean
Honorary titles:	Sir	Lord
	Lady	Madame

- Capitalize all parts of a compound title.

     Vice President   Lieutenant Governor

- Capitalize titles to show respect.

     The Senator spoke to us at the ribbon cutting.

     A senator's time is always in demand.

- Capitalize titles used in direct address.

     Doctor, I have a pain in my side.

     Nurse, please bring me the bandage.

Quick Tip

Always defer to a person's preference in the capitalization of his or her name.

3. Capitalize titles that show family relationships when the title is used with a person's name or in direct address.

   Grandmother Pirandello came from Italy in the 1950s.

   Grandfather, will you take us to the zoo?

4. Capitalize titles of parents and relatives not preceded by a possessive word (such as *my*).

   We saw Mother kissing Santa Claus.

   I saw my mother kissing my father.

5. Capitalize abbreviations that appear after a person's name.

   Martin Luther King, Jr.

   Laurie Rozakis, Ph.D.

   Grace Lui, M.D.

6. Capitalize the major words in titles of books, plays, movies, newspapers, and magazines.

   Do not capitalize the articles: *a, an, the*

   Do not capitalize prepositions: *at, by, for, of, in, up, on, so, on, to,* etc.

   Do not capitalize conjunctions: *and, as, but, if, or, nor*

   In effect, any word with more than four letters in a title gets capitalized.

   - Capitalize book titles.

     Grammar and Usage for the Utterly Confused

     Schaum's Quick Guide to Writing Great Research Papers

   - Capitalize play titles.

     She Stoops to Conquer

     Cats

   - Capitalize movie titles.

     The Great Escape

     From Here to Eternity

   - Capitalize newspaper titles.

     The New York Times

     The Washington Post

   - Capitalize magazine titles.

     Sports Illustrated for Kids

     Atlantic Monthly

7. Capitalize acronyms.

   An *acronym* is an abbreviation formed from the first letter of each word in the title. A few words have entered English that were first acronyms but are now formed with lowercase letters, such as *laser* and *radar*. However, most acronyms are formed with capital letters. *Note:* Since acronyms are used as words, they never take periods.

NATO (North Atlantic Treaty Organization)

NASA (National Aeronautics and Space Administration)

Capitalize Names of Places and Events

1. Capitalize names of geographical places and sections of the country.

   Europe   Asia   United States of America

   Lake Superior   Venus   Yellowstone National Park

2. Capitalize a compass point when it identifies a specific area of the country.

   We live in the South.

   The West is still wild and untamed.

3. Don't capitalize a compass point when it refers to direction.

   The storm is coming from the south.

   Drive west 4 miles and turn left at the shopping center.

4. Capitalize the names of specific historical events, eras, and documents.

   the Revolutionary War Reconstruction

   the Declaration of Independence   the Gettysburg Address

Capitalize Names of Languages and Religions

1. Capitalize the names of languages, nationalities, countries, and ethnic and racial identifications.

Language	Nationalities	Countries	Ethnicities
French	Japanese	Pakistan	African-American
German	Australian	India	Native American
Italian	Iranian	Bosnia	South African

Quick Tip

Should you always capitalize the names of countries and languages? Should it be *french fries* or *French Fries? spanish omelet* or *Spanish omelet?* No one's in agreement, so pick one style and stick with it.

---

2. Capitalize religions and references to the Supreme Being, including the pronouns referring to the Supreme Being.

   Christianity, Hindu, Catholicism, Judaism

   the Creator, Him, He, Heaven, His name

   Don't capitalize the words *god* or *goddess* when they refer to ancient mythology.

   the goddess Athena

   the god Hermes

Capitalize Proper Adjectives and Product Names

1. Capitalize proper adjectives formed from proper nouns.

Proper Nouns	Proper Adjectives
Italy	Italian
Rome	Roman
Alps	Alpine
Newton	Newtonian

- In a hyphenated proper adjective, capitalize only the adjective.

  Spanish-speaking residents

- Don't capitalize the prefix attached to a proper adjective unless the prefix refers to a nationality.

  all-American   Old English

2. Capitalize brand names and trademarks.

   Jell-O pudding   Kleenex tissues

   Freon   Band-Aid

   Fresca   Xerox

Capitalize Names of Organizations, Institutions, Courses, and Famous Buildings

Since names of organizations, institutions, courses, and famous buildings are all proper nouns, they get capitalized.

Do not capitalize the articles: *a, an, the.*

Do not capitalize prepositions: *at, by, for, of, in, up, on, so, on, to,* etc.

Do not capitalize conjunctions: *and, as, but, if, or, nor.*

1. Capitalize the names of organizations.

   The Boy Scouts of America   Rotary International

   The Red Cross   General Motors

2. Capitalize the names of institutions.

   Lincoln Center for the Performing Arts

   The United Nations

3. Capitalize the names of courses.

   Introduction to Biology (but not biology)

   Mathematics 203 (but not mathematics)

4. Capitalize the names of buildings.

   The Empire State Building   the Sears Tower

Capitalize Names of Days, Months, and Holidays

Again, these are all proper nouns, so they are all capitalized.

1. Capitalize names of days.

   Monday   Tuesday

   Wednesday   Sunday

2. Capitalize names of months.

   February   March

   April   July

3. Capitalize names of holidays.

   Thanksgiving   Kwanzaa

   Passover   Ramadan

Capitalize Time and Other Proper Nouns

1. Capitalize abbreviations for time.

    6:00 A.M.　　　7:00 P.M.

2. Capitalize names of celestial bodies, except the moon and the sun.

    the Milky Way　　　the Big Dipper

    Capitalize the earth only when it is used as a planet.

    The Earth is not flat.

3. Capitalize names of awards.

    the Nobel Peace Prize　the Caldecott Medal

4. Capitalize the words I and O.

    Quickly, I turned around.

    O! Did you see that?

Capitalize the First Word of . . .

1. A sentence

    The shortest presidential inaugural address was George Washington's, at 135 words.

    The longest was by William Henry Harrison, at 8,445 words.

2. A complete sentence after a colon

    Only two U.S. presidents and their wives are buried at Arlington National Cemetery: John F. Kennedy and his wife Jacqueline Kennedy Onassis and William Taft and his wife Helen Heron Taft are buried there.

3. A quotation, if it is a complete sentence.

    The teacher said, "Abraham Lincoln lost eight elections for various offices before winning the election in 1860."

    but

    "Abraham Lincoln lost eight elections for various offices," the teacher said, "before winning the election in 1860."

4. A line of poetry

    Shall I compare thee to a summer's day?
    Thou art more lovely and more temperate.
    Rough winds do shake the darling buds of May,
    And summer's lease hath all too short a date.
    Sometimes too hot the eye of heaven shines,
    And often is his gold complexion dimm'd;

And every fair from fair sometimes declines,
By chance or nature's changing course untrimm'd;
But thy eternal summer shall not fade
Nor lose possession of that fair thou ow'st;
Nor shall Death brag thou wander'st in his shade,
When in eternal lines to time thou grow'st:
So long as men can breathe or eyes can see,
So long lives this, and this gives life to thee.

Quick Tip

In poetry and old-fashioned novels, words are sometimes capitalized for emphasis. In this Shakespearean sonnet, for example, "Death" is capitalized to personify it: to make it seem like a living being. Today, however, words are capitalized for emphasis only in e-mail.

---

5. The greeting of a letter
   Dear Mr. Plotnick:
   To Whom It May Concern:
   Dear Mom,

6. The complimentary close of a letter. Notice that only the first word is capitalized, not subsequent words in a phrase.
   Yours very truly,   Sincerely yours,

7. Each item in an outline
   I. Greek architecture
      A. Greek temples
      B. Greek theaters and amphitheaters
      C. Greek colonnades

8. Each item in a list

1. Evaluate the performance of our new meters
   This report is designed to:

2. Expand the data base

3. Evaluate data

4. Make recommendations

Good Things Come in Small Packages: The Rules of Abbreviations

An *abbreviation* is a shortened form of a word or phrase. Abbreviations start with a capital letter and end with a period. They are a handy way to save time and space when you're writing, but only if you use commonly accepted abbreviations. Otherwise, you'll just confuse your readers. Here is how to use abbreviations correctly.

1. Abbreviate social titles and titles of rank, both before and after a person's name.
   Mr.   Mrs.   Ms.   Dr.

Quick Tip

Miss is a title that comes before a person's name, but since it isn't an abbreviation, it doesn't have a period at the end. A usage note: Many women now prefer the title "Ms.," but some still prefer "Miss." When in doubt, ask the woman what title she prefers.

---

2. Abbreviate names of academic degrees.
   Jonathan Hernandez, B.A. (Bachelor of Arts)
   Hi-Jing Yu, M.F.A. (Master of Fine Arts)

Because of their Latin roots, abbreviations for many degrees can be written in either direction: M.A. or A.M. for Masters of Arts, for instance. The following chart shows some of the most commonly abbreviated degrees:

Degree	Abbreviation
Bachelor of Science	B.A.
Bachelor of Business Administration	B.B.A.
Masters of Arts	M.A. or A.M.
Masters of Science	M.S. or S.M.
Masters of Business Administration	M.B.A.
Medical Doctor	M.D.
Doctor of Philosophy	Ph.D.
Doctor of Divinity	D.D.
Doctor of Dental Surgery	D.D.S.
Registered Nurse	R.N.

3. Abbreviate time.

A.M. (before noon; *ante meridian*)

P.M. (afternoon; *post meridian*)

4. Abbreviate some historical periods. In most—but not all—cases, the abbreviation is placed after the date.

Ancient times (2,000 years in the past)

B.C. (before the birth of Christ)

B.C.E. (before the common era)

Modern times (within the last 2,000 years)

C.E. (common era)

A.D. (*Anno Domini,* "in the year of the Lord," an abbreviation that comes before the date)

Here's how these abbreviations are used:

Emperor Augustus lived from 63 B.C. (or B.C.E.) to A.D. 14 (or C.E.).

5. Abbreviate geographical terms.

Sammi lives on Woodlawn Dr.

The following chart lists the most common abbreviations for geographical terms.

Place	Abbreviation
Avenue	Ave.
Boulevard	Blvd.
Drive	Dr.
Fort	Ft.
Mountain	Mt.
Point	Pt.
Road	Rd.
Route	Rte.
Square	Sq.
Street	St.

6. Abbreviate names of states.

Use the official U.S. Post Office zip code abbreviations, which are not followed by periods. There's a list of all 50 abbreviations in your telephone book.

FL (Florida)   PA (Pennsylvania)

7. Abbreviate some Latin expressions.

e.g. (for example)   et al. (and others)

8. Abbreviate measurements.

inches is abbreviated in.   feet is abbreviated ft.

Here are some of the most common abbreviations for measurements. Note that metric abbreviations are not followed by a period.

Item	Abbreviation
yards	yd.
miles	mi.
teaspoon	tsp.
tablespoon	tbs.
ounce	oz.
pound	lb.
pint	pt.
quart	qt.
Fahrenheit	F.
Celsius	C
grams	g
kilograms	kg
millimeters	mm
liters	L
centimeters	cm
meters	m
kilometers	km

9. Abbreviate the titles of some organizations and things.

These abbreviations are not followed by a period.

UN (United Nations)

FBI (Federal Bureau of Investigation)

TV (television)

It's a Wrap

✔ Capital letters are important because they help determine meaning in written language.

✔ Capitalize all proper nouns and proper adjectives.

✔ Capitalize the first word at the beginning of a sentence.

✔ Most abbreviations start with a capital letter and end with a period. Use only commonly accepted abbreviations.

Test Yourself

QUESTIONS

True-False Questions

1. Capitalize all proper nouns.
2. Capitalize proper names and names of geographical places, specific historical events, eras, documents, languages, nationalities, countries, and races.
3. Capitalize the first word at the beginning of a sentence.
4. It's not important to use capital letters consistently within a particular document.
5. Capitalize only the last part of a person's name.
6. If a name begins with *d', de,* or *du,* do not capitalize the prefix unless it is preceded by a first name or a title.
7. A person can always decide how to capitalize the words in his or her name.
8. Do not capitalize the names of any animals.
9. A personal name that is used as a common noun is capitalized, as in "Watt" and "Kelvin."
10. Capitalize titles used before a person's name.
11. Capitalize only the first part of a compound title, as in "Vice president."
12. Capitalize titles that show family relationships when the title is used with a person's name or in direct address.
13. Capitalize titles of parents and relatives not preceded by a possessive word (such as *my*).
14. Capitalize the major words in titles of books, plays, movies, newspapers, and magazines.
15. Do not capitalize *acronyms,* abbreviations formed from the first letter of each word in a phrase.
16. Capitalize a compass point when it identifies a specific area of the country or refers to direction.
17. Capitalize religions and references to the Supreme Being, including the pronouns referring to the Supreme Being.
18. Capitalize proper adjectives formed from proper nouns. Always capitalize the prefix attached to a proper adjective.
19. An *abbreviation* is a shortened form of a word or phrase. Abbreviations start with a capital letter and end with a period.
20. Abbreviate social titles and titles of rank, academic degrees, and some historical periods.

Completion Questions

Select the word that best completes each sentence.

1. The reception will be held at the (vanderbilt, Vanderbilt) at 8:00 (p.m., P.M.).

2. The (Crab Nebula, crab nebula) star cluster was visible in the sky from our (Balcony, balcony).

3. The children's book (author, Author) was thrilled to win a (McArthur, MCArthur, Mcarthur) Fellowship.

4. After the explosion, (I, i) quickly took cover.

5. The letter began (dear Ms. Snodgrass, Dear ms. Snodgrass, Dear Ms. Snodgrass).

6. The letter ended (Yours Very truly, yours very truly, Yours very truly,).

7. The (commencement, Commencement) speaker was Reggie Monsanto, (M.A., m.a.).

8. The bones dated back to 2,000 (b.C., B.C.).

9. We looked at apartments on Waverly (Blvd., blvd.). Smith (ste. Str., St.), and Dorothy (Dr., dr.)

10. The lumber was 4 (FT, ft., Fte.) long.

Multiple-Choice Questions

Select the best revision for each sentence.

1. The only four countries that start with the letter "D" are denmark, djibouti, dominica, and the dominican Republic.
   - (a) The only four Countries that start with the letter "D" are Denmark, Djibouti, Dominica, and the Dominican Republic.
   - (b) The only four countries that start with the letter "D" are Denmark, Djibouti, Dominica, and the Dominican republic.
   - (c) The only four Countries that start with the letter "D" are denmark, djibouti, dominica, and the dominican Republic.
   - (d) the only four countries that start with the letter "D" are Denmark, Djibouti, Dominica, and the dominican Republic.

2. When first lady eleanor roosevelt received an alarming number of threatening letters soon after her husband became president at the height of the depression, the secret service insisted that she carry a pistol in her purse.
   - (a) When first lady Eleanor Roosevelt received an alarming number of threatening letters soon after her husband became president at the height of the Depression, the Secret Service insisted that she carry a pistol in her purse.
   - (b) When First lady Eleanor Roosevelt received an alarming number of threatening letters soon after her husband became President at the height of the depression, the secret service insisted that she carry a pistol in her purse.
   - (c) When First Lady Eleanor Roosevelt received an alarming number of threatening letters soon after her husband became President at the height of the Depression, the Secret Service insisted that she carry a pistol in her purse.
   - (d) When First lady Eleanor Roosevelt received an alarming number of threatening letters soon after her husband became president at the height of the Depression, the secret service insisted that she carry a pistol in her purse.

3. Winston churchill, Franklin delano Roosevelt, Theodore Roosevelt, and Eleanor Roosevelt were all Cousins through one connection or another.

   (a) Winston Churchill, Franklin Delano Roosevelt, Theodore Roosevelt, and Eleanor Roosevelt were all cousins through one connection or another.

   (b) Winston Churchill, Franklin delano Roosevelt, Theodore Roosevelt, and Eleanor Roosevelt were all cousins through one connection or another.

   (c) Winston churchill, Franklin delano roosevelt, theodore Roosevelt, and eleanor Roosevelt were all cousins through one connection or another.

   (d) Winston Churchill, Franklin Delano Roosevelt, Theodore Roosevelt, and Eleanor Roosevelt were all Cousins through one connection or another.

4. After the civil war, the u.s. sued great britain for damages that were caused by them building ships for the confederacy.

   (a) After the Civil War, the U.S. sued Great Britain for damages that were caused by them building ships for the Confederacy.

   (b) After the civil war, the U.S. sued Great Britain for damages that were caused by them building ships for the Confederacy.

   (c) After the Civil War, the U.S. sued Great britain for damages that were caused by them building ships for the Confederacy.

   (d) After the Civil war, the U.S. sued Great Britain for damages that were caused by them building ships for the confederacy.

5. The U.S. originally asked for $1 Billion but settled on $25 Million.

   (a) The U.S. originally asked for $1 billion but settled on $25 Million.

   (b) The U.S. originally asked for $1 billion but settled on $25 million.

   (c) The u.s. originally asked for $1 Billion but settled on $25 Million.

   (d) the U.s. originally asked for $1 billion but settled on $25 million.

6. John quincy Adams took his last skinny-dip in the potomac on his Seventy-Ninth birthday.

   (a) John quincy Adams took his last skinny-dip in the Potomac on his seventy-ninth birthday.

   (b) John Quincy Adams took his last skinny-dip in the Potomac on his seventy-ninth birthday.

   (c) John Quincy Adams took his last skinny-dip in the potomac on his seventy-ninth birthday.

   (d) John Quincy adams took his last skinny-dip in the Potomac on his Seventy-ninth birthday.

7. The panama canal was excavated from the coasts inland; the final short segment was cleared by explosives detonated by president Woodrow Wilson, who sent the signal by wire from New York city.

   (a) The Panama canal was excavated from the coasts inland; the final short segment was cleared by explosives detonated by President woodrow Wilson, who sent the signal by wire from New york City.

(b) The panama Canal was excavated from the coasts inland; the final short segment was cleared by explosives detonated by President Woodrow Wilson, who sent the signal by wire from new york city.

(c) The Panama Canal was excavated from the coasts inland; the final short segment was cleared by explosives detonated by President Woodrow Wilson, who sent the signal by wire from New York City.

(d) The Panama canal was excavated from the Coasts inland; the final short segment was cleared by explosives detonated by president Woodrow Wilson, who sent the signal by wire from New York city.

8. When john wilkes booth leaped onto the stage after shooting the president, he tripped—on the american flag.

(a) When John Wilkes Booth leaped onto the stage after shooting the President, he tripped—on the American flag.

(b) When John wilkes Booth leaped onto the stage after shooting the President, he tripped—on the American flag.

(c) When John Wilkes Booth leaped onto the stage after shooting the President, he tripped—on the American Flag.

(d) when John Wilkes Booth leaped onto the stage after shooting The President, he tripped—on the American Flag.

9. robert todd lincoln, son of president abraham lincoln, was present at the assassinations of three u.s. presidents: lincoln, garfield, and mckinley.

(a) Robert todd Lincoln, Son of President Abraham Lincoln, was present at the assassinations of three U.S. presidents: Lincoln, Garfield, and McKinley.

(b) Robert Todd Lincoln, son of president Abraham Lincoln, was present at the assassinations of three U.S. presidents: Lincoln, Garfield, and MCKinley.

(c) Robert Todd Lincoln, son of President Abraham Lincoln, was present at the assassinations of three U.S. presidents: lincoln, garfield, and MCKinley.

(d) Robert Todd Lincoln, son of President Abraham Lincoln, was present at the assassinations of three U.S. presidents: Lincoln, Garfield, and McKinley.

10. james k. polk was the only president to have been speaker of the house.

(a) James k. Polk was the only President to have been Speaker of the House.

(b) James K. Polk was the only president to have been Speaker Of The House.

(c) James k. Polk was the only President to have been Speaker Of The House.

(d) James K. Polk was the only President to have been Speaker of the House.

ANSWER KEY

True-False Questions

1. T   2. T   3. T   4. F   5. F   6. F   7. T   8. F   9. F   10. T   11. F   12. T
13. T   14. T   15. F   16. F   17. T   18. F   19. T   20. T

Completion Questions

1. Vanderbilt, P.M.   2. Crab Nebula, balcony   3. author, McArthur   4. I
5. Dear Ms. Snodgrass   6. Yours very truly,   7. commencement, M.A.   8. B.C.
9. Blvd., St., Dr.   10. ft.

Multiple-Choice Questions

1. b   2. c   3. a   4. a   5. b   6. b   7. c   8. a   9. d   10. d

PART 5

Struttin'
Your Stuff
with Style

CHAPTER 12

Developing Your Own Writing Style

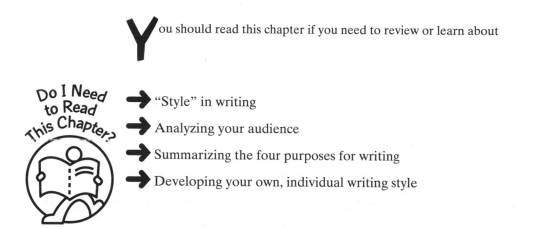

You should read this chapter if you need to review or learn about

Do I Need to Read This Chapter?

➡ "Style" in writing

➡ Analyzing your audience

➡ Summarizing the four purposes for writing

➡ Developing your own, individual writing style

Get Started

In this chapter, you will delve into the importance of suiting your writing style to your audience, purpose, and topic.

What is *Style* in Writing?

Consider the following three passages. As you read them, think about what qualities make them the same and different from each other.

Passage 1

It was the best of times, it was the worst of times, it was the age of wisdom, it was the age of foolishness, it was the epoch of belief, it was the epoch of incredulity, it was the season of Light, it was the season of Darkness, it was the spring of hope, it was the winter of despair, we had everything before us, we had nothing before us, we were all going direct to Heaven, we were all going direct the other way—in short, the period was so far like the present period, that some of its noisiest authorities insisted on its being received, for good or for evil, in the superlative degree of comparison only. (Charles Dickens, *A Tale of Two Cities*)

Passage 2

It is a truth universally acknowledged, that a single man in possession of a good fortune, must be in want of a wife.

However little known the feelings or views of such a man must be on his first entering a neighborhood, this truth is so well fixed in the minds of the surrounding families, that he is considered as the rightful property of some one or other of their daughters.

"My dear Mr. Bennet," said his lady to him one day, "have you heard that Netherfield Park is to be let at last?"

Mr. Bennet replied that he had not.

"But it is," returned she; "for Mrs. Long has just been here, and she told me all about it."

Mr. Bennet made no answer.

"Do you not want to know who has taken it?" cried his wife impatiently.

"*You* want to tell me, and I have no objection to hearing it." (Jane Austen, *Pride and Prejudice*)

Passage 3

Simple everyday upkeep will help maintain the beauty of your new carpet. One important aspect of this care is cleaning up food and beverage spills quickly and correctly. Follow these steps:

1. Blot up as much of the spill as possible. Use a clean, white cloth or white paper towels. Try to work quickly so the liquid does not have time to penetrate the carpet.
2. If the carpet is stained, blot down with a cloth moistened with warm water. Do not use hot water; it will set the stain. Press down firmly to remove as much liquid as you can. Do not rub the stain, because rubbing can change the texture of the carpet. Continue blotting with clean cloths or paper towels until the stain is gone.
3. If the stain does not disappear, mix 1 quart warm water with 1 teaspoon mild liquid laundry detergent. Do not use dishwashing detergent or any detergent that contains bleach. Cover the stain with the cleaner. Let it sit five minutes. Then blot up the liquid with clean white cloths or paper towels.

4. Rinse the stained area with warm water and blot until the carpet is almost dry. Cover the stain with a few layers of paper towels or cloths.

5. When the carpet is completely dry, vacuum the carpet. To restore the texture, you may then wish to brush the carpet gently.

6. Deep stains may need a professional stain remover. This can be obtained from your local hardware or carpet store. Follow the directions on the container. If you need additional assistance, call 800-555-CLEAN. (From a carpet care manual)

Passages 1 and 2 are similar because they are both parts of novels. As a result, they both tell a story. The authors aim to entertain their readers. Passage 3, in contrast, does not tell a story. Rather, it gives directions. As a result, its purpose is to instruct.

Now look a little deeper: Passage 1 has long sentences. Looking more closely, you can see that the entire passage is one single very long sentence! Dickens also uses parallel structure as he matches phrases and clauses. The words are elevated, too, as shown in his choice of the word *epoch,* for example. There's no dialogue, however.

Passage 2 also has long sentences, but they are nowhere near as long as the sentence Dickens uses. The diction is British, as shown in the word *let* used for *rented.* This passage is developed through dialogue.

Both passages are witty. There's no humor at all in Passage 3, however!

The Elements of Style

As this analysis reveals, different writers have their own distinctive way of writing. A writer's *style* is his or her distinctive way of writing. Style is a series of choices, shown on the following chart.

Element of Style	Examples
Description	Words that appeal to the five senses
Dialogue	Showing a character's exact words in quotation marks
Figures of speech	Similes, metaphors, hyperbole
Parallel structure	Matching words, phrases, and clauses
Punctuation	Commas, semicolons, colons, dashes
Purpose	To entertain, to instruct, to persuade, to explain
Sentence length	Short sentences, middle-length sentences, long sentences
Sentence structure	Questions, statements, exclamations, commands
Tone	Humorous, somber, serious, eerie, matter-of-fact
Topic	Subject of the writing
Voice	Author's stance toward the material
Words	Slang, vernacular, everyday speech, elevated diction

Style can be described in many ways, including

formal	informal	stiff	grand	allusive
elevated	academic	relaxed	heroic	ironic
colloquial	breezy	familiar	rich	serious
technical	sensory	abstract	plain	ornate

Some professional writers celebrated for their distinctive writing style include Jane Austen, Ernest Hemingway, Truman Capote, John McPhee, Tracy Kidder, and E. B. White. (Some criticized for their writing style include James Joyce, Theodore Dreiser, F. Scott Fitzgerald, and Charles Dickens!)

A clear writing style is not restricted to professional writers, however. Everyday people get ahead in part because of their ability to write clearly and effectively. For example,

- Accountants must write clear cover letters for audits.
- Computer specialists write proposals.
- Educators write observations of staff members and reports on students.
- Engineers write reports, e-mails, and faxes.
- Insurance brokers write letters soliciting business.
- Lawyers need to make their briefs logical.
- Marketing personnel do sales reports.
- Retail workers often write letters of recommendation and promotion.
- Stock and bond traders write letters and prospectuses.

Everyone writes resumes, cover letters, memos, faxes, and business letters. Therefore, we all need to develop an effective writing style that helps us get our point across clearly, concisely, and gracefully.

While everyone's writing style is as individual as his or her fingerprints, every writing style shares the same characteristics:

- It suits the tone to the readers. For example, you would use a respectful tone in a eulogy (funeral speech), but you could use a humorous tone in a speech at a birthday party.
- It is free of errors in grammar and usage (unless fragments are being used in dialogue).
- It is free of errors in spelling and punctuation (unless misspellings are being used in dialect).
- It does not include offensive words.

Writers often change their style for different kinds of writing and to suit different audiences. In poetry, for example, an author might use more imagery than he or she would use in prose. Dr. Seuss wrote whimsical novels such as *The Cat in the Hat* for children, as well as effective advertisements for Burma Shave! E. B. White wrote the children's classics *Charlotte's Web, Stuart Little,* and *The Trumpet of the Swan,* as well as essays for adults collected under the title *Is Sex Dead?* The style of each publication is clearly different, yet each can be equally well written. As these examples show, writing style is first adjusted to satisfy your *audience.*

Quick Tip

Unless you've been granted the gift of an exceptionally fluent tongue, writing as you talk usually results in awkward and repetitive documents. Most of us hesitate as we speak to allow us time to gather our thoughts. We also backtrack to pick up points we might have missed on the first go-round. As a result, a document written "by ear" usually sounds illogical.

Audience and Style

A writer's audience are the people who read what you have written. To be an effective writer and speaker, you must understand how your *audience* is likely to react to what you say and how you say it. Knowing *who* you are communicating with is fundamental to the success of any message. You need to tailor your writing style to suit the audience's needs, interests, and goals.

Before you write anything that you wish to share with others, analyze your audience. Ask yourself these questions:

1. Who will be reading what I have written?
   Possible audiences include teachers, classmates, colleagues, clients, friends, strangers.

2. How much do my readers know about my topic at this point?
   Are they novices, experts, or somewhere in between?

3. What information must I provide for my message to be successful?
   Sometimes you will have to provide a great deal of information to help your readers grasp your message. Other times, in contrast, you'll have little, or no, information to add.

4. How does my audience feel about this topic?
   Are they neutral, hostile, enthusiastic, or somewhere in between? A hostile audience is much more difficult to reach than a friendly one.

5. What obstacles (if any) must I overcome for my message to be successful?
   You might have to deliver bad news, for instance.

6. What style of writing does my audience anticipate and prefer?
   Of course, you will suit your style to your audience's needs and expectations. For instance, you wouldn't use long, difficult words for young children. Similarly, you wouldn't use many idioms (nonliteral phrases) for nonnative speakers of English.

A note on audience: In most instances, you will have a clearly defined audience, so you can adjust your style to appeal to them and help you achieve your purpose. Other times, however, your audience won't be as easy to identify. For instance, you might be sending a resume and cover letter to a job identified by only the most general description and a post office box. In this situation, it's even more critical to get some information about your readers. You might first send a query letter asking for more details, for instance.

Purpose and Style

A love letter. A business memo. A short story. A poem. An inventory. A letter to the IRS explaining a problem with a tax return.

Although each of these documents seems very different, they are alike in one crucial way: They each have a clear purpose. *Keeping your purpose in mind as you write helps you craft a clear and appropriate style.*

We appear to write for many reasons, but remarkably, there are only four purposes for writing:

- To explain
- To persuade
- To describe
- To tell a story

The following chart explains purpose in writing.

Purpose	Definition	Examples	
Exposition	To explain To show To tell	Manuals Recipes Business letters Term papers Textbooks	News stories Press releases Reports Wills Articles
Persuasion	To convince	Critical reviews Resumes Job evaluations Letters to the editor Speeches	Editorials Cover letters Letters of recommendation Letters of complaint
Description	To describe	Poems	Journals
Narration	To tell a story	Autobiographies Anecdotes Short stories	Biographies Oral histories Novels

A document often has more than one purpose, but one purpose usually dominates. For example, a letter of complaint will describe, explain, and persuade. However, its primary purpose is to persuade, as you try to convince your audience to make redress.

Developing Your Style

As you learned earlier in this chapter, style is made up of many elements. These include sentences, especially their length and structure. Style is also created by description, repetition, voice, parallel structure, and punctuation. Now,

1. Style and sentences

   Let's look at these stylistic elements in greater detail.

   - Suit your sentence length to your topic. When your topic is complicated or full of numbers, use short, simple sentences to aid understanding. When your topic is less complex, use longer sentences with subordination to show how ideas are linked together and to avoid repetition.

   - Clear writing uses sentences of different lengths and types to create variety and interest. Craft your sentences to express your ideas in the best possible way. Mix *simple, compound, complex,* and *compound-complex* sentences for a more effective style. Review Chapters 8 and 9 for a complete discussion of the four sentence types.

   - Overall, vary the length of your sentences. The unbroken rhythm of monotonous sentence length creates a dull style.

   - Select the subject of each sentence based on what you want to emphasize. Since readers focus on the subject of your sentence, make it the most important aspect of each thought.

2. Style and description

   - Add adjectives and adverbs to a sentence (when suitable) for emphasis and variety. Expand sentences with adjectives and adverbs. When you want to avoid a very brief sentence, add modifiers. Base your decision to expand a sentence on its focus and how it works in the context of surrounding sentences.

   - Use verbs rather than nouns to communicate your ideas. This makes your writing more forceful and less wordy. For example, replace forms of *to be* with action verbs, as the following example shows:

     Weak: The advantages of shopping ahead *is* saving time and money.

     Improved: Shopping ahead *will save* you time and money.

Quick Tip

There will be times when you'll have to use "big words," especially if they are technical terms or necessary jargon. Much of the time, however, big words just set up barriers between you and your audience. Instead, always choose words that suit your purpose and audience.

3. Style and repetition

Repeat key words or ideas to achieve emphasis. Only repeat the words that contain a main idea or that use rhythm to focus attention on a main idea. Repetition is a key element in many of our most famous speeches, such as John F. Kennedy's inaugural address. Kennedy used repetition to capture the cadences of natural speech to create one of the most memorable lines of the twentieth century: "And so, my fellow Americans, ask not what your country can do for you—ask what you can do for your country."

4. Style and voice

- Use the active voice, not the passive voice, as you learned in earlier chapters.

- In informal writing, use the pronoun *you* to engage your readers. The second-person pronoun *you* (rather than the third-person *he, she, one*) gives your writing more impact because it directly addresses the reader, as this example shows:

    Weak: Deductions from *one's* account will be posted on the first of the month.

    Improved: Deductions from *your* account will be posted on the first of the month.

5. Style and punctuation

Your choice of punctuation also has a critical influence on your writing style because it determines the degree of linkage between sentences. Further, it suggests whether sentence elements are coordinating or subordinating. Here are some guidelines:

- Use a period to show a full separation between ideas. However, be aware that a series of short, declarative sentences often creates a tense and choppy style.

- Use a comma and a coordinating conjunction to show the following relationships: addition, choice, consequence, contrast, or cause.

- Use a semicolon to show that the second sentence completes the content of the first sentence. The semicolon suggests a link but leaves it to the reader to make the connection.

- Use a semicolon and a conjunctive adverb (a word such as *nevertheless, however,* etc.) to show the relationship between ideas: *addition, consequence, contrast, cause and effect, time, emphasis, or addition.*

It's a Wrap

✔ Style is a person's distinctive way of writing.

✔ Always tailor your style to suit your audience, your readers.

✔ Also consider your purpose—to entertain, to explain, to tell a story, to persuade.

✔ Create *style* through your choices, including words, sentence length, sentence structure, and punctuation.

Test Yourself

QUESTIONS

True-False Questions

1. Style is found only in fiction such as novels and short stories; nonfiction writing does not have a distinctive style.

2. Only professional writers can develop a clear and distinctive writing style.

3. People in all walks of life can get ahead in part because of their ability to write clearly and effectively.

4. The ability to write well is something you are born with, like being right- or left-handed.

5. Everyone's writing style is as individual as his or her fingerprints, but every writing style shares many of the same characteristics.

6. In poetry, a writer might use more imagery than he or she would use in prose.

7. As a general rule, you should write just as you speak.

8. You need to adapt your writing style to suit the readers' needs, interests, and goals.

9. Before you write anything that you wish to share with others, analyze your audience.

10. A writing rarely has more than one purpose, and the purpose is always clear and obvious.

11. Suit your sentence length to your topic; for example, when your topic is complicated or full of numbers, use short, simple sentences to aid understanding.

12. Use nouns rather than verbs to communicate your ideas.

13. Repeat key words or ideas to achieve emphasis.

14. However, only repeat the words that contain a main idea or that use rhythm to focus attention on a main idea.

15. When it comes to creating an effective and distinctive writing style, punctuation does not matter a great deal.

Completion Questions

Select the word that best completes each sentence.

1. A writer's *style* is his or her distinctive way of (thinking, writing).

2. All good writing is clear and (correct, perfect).

3. Writers often change their style for different kinds of writing and to suit different (readers, moods).

4. A writer's (*diction, audience*) are the people who read what he or she has written.

5. Keeping your purpose in mind as you write helps you craft a clear and appropriate (audience, style).

6. Expository writing (convinces readers, explains a topic).

7. Narrative writing (tells a story, proves a point).

8. Your Last Will and Testament is an example of writing that (explains, persuades, narrates).

9. (Effective, Confusing) writing uses sentences of different lengths and types to create variety and interest.

10. Select the (subject, predicate) of each sentence based on what you want to emphasize.

11. Unless you want to avoid assigning blame or you do not know the subject of a sentence, use the (active, passive) voice rather than the (active, passive) voice.

12. When writing informally, use the pronoun (*one, you*) to engage your readers.

13. Your choice of (modifiers, punctuation) also has a critical influence on your writing style because it determines the degree of linkage between sentences.

14. Use a (comma, semicolon) if you wish to show that the second sentence completes the content of the first sentence.

15. Use a semicolon and a conjunctive (adverb, adjective)—a word such as *nevertheless* or *however*—to show the relationship between ideas.

Multiple-Choice Questions

Choose the best answer to each question.

1. Style includes all the following elements except
    (a) Description
    (b) Dialogue
    (c) Metaphors
    (d) Audience

2. Which of the following is the best definition of description?
    (a) Words that appeal to the five senses
    (b) A character's exact words in quotation marks
    (c) Matching words, phrases, and clauses
    (d) The subject of the writing

3. How many purposes are there for writing?
    (a) Four
    (b) Three
    (c) Two
    (d) One

4. Figures of speech include all the following *except*
    (a) Metaphors
    (b) Similes
    (c) Voice
    (d) Personification

5. The *tone* of Stephen King's novels and short stories is best described as
    (a) Humorous
    (b) Creepy and spooky
    (c) Slang
    (d) Vernacular

6. All effective writing shares every one of the following characteristics *except*
    (a) Clarity
    (b) An effective tone that suits the writer's audience and purpose

(c) An awareness of the conventions of standard written English

(d) Any words the writer wants to use

7. All the following are examples of expository writing *except*

    (a) Encyclopedia entry

    (b) Letter of recommendation

    (c) Front-page newspaper story

    (d) Recipe

8. All the following are examples of narrative writing *except*

    (a) Short story

    (b) Novel

    (c) Newspaper editorial

    (d) Funny joke

9. Your resume is best described as an example of

    (a) Narrative writing

    (b) Descriptive writing

    (c) Expository writing

    (d) Persuasive writing

10. Use a comma and a coordinating conjunction to show *all* of the following relationships *except*

    (a) Contradiction

    (b) Consequence

    (c) Choice

    (d) Addition

Further Exercises

Describe the style in each passage:

1. What, then, is the American, this new man? He is neither a European nor the descendent of an European; hence that strange mixture of blood, which you will find in no other country. I could point out to you a family whose grandfather was an Englishman, whose wife was Dutch, whose son married a French woman, and whose present four sons now have four wives of different nations. *He* is an American who, leaving behind all his ancient prejudices and manners, received new ones from the new mode of life he has embraced, the new government he obeys, and the new ranks he holds. He becomes an American by being received in the broad lap of our great Alma Mater. Here individuals of all nations are melted into a new race of men, whose labors and posterity will one day cause great changes in the world. Americans are the western pilgrims who are carrying along with them that great mass of arts, sciences, vigor, and industry which began long since in the East; they will finish the great circle. The Americans were once scattered all over Europe; here they are incorporated into one of the finest systems of population

which has ever appeared, and which thereafter become distinct by the power of different climates they inhabit. The American ought therefore to love this country much better than that wherein he or his forefathers were born. Here the rewards of his industry follow with equal steps the progress of his labor; his labor is founded on the basis of nature, self-interest; can it want a stronger allurement? . . . The American is a new man, who acts upon new principles; he must therefore entertain new ideas and form new opinions. (Hector St. John de Crevecoeur, "What is an American?")

2. And one example, whether love or fear doth work more in a child for virtue and learning, I will gladly report; which may be heard with some pleasure and followed with more profit. Before I went into Germany, I came to Broadgate to take my leave of that noble Lady Jane Grey . . . "And how came you, madame," quoth I, "to this deep knowledge of pleasure, and what did chiefly allure you unto it, seeing not many women, but very few men, have attained thereunto?" "I will tell you," quoth she, "and tell you a truth which perchance ye will marvel at. One of the great benefits that ever God gave me is that he sent me so sharp and severe parents and so gentle a schoolmaster. For when I am in presence either of father or mother, whether I speak, keep silence, sit, stand, or go, eat, drink, be merry or sad, be sewing, playing, dancing, or doing anything else, I must do it, as it were, in such weight, measure, and number, even so perfectly as God made the world, or else I am so sharply taunted, so cruelly threatened, yea, presently sometimes, with pinches, nips, and bobs, and other ways which I will not name for the honor I bear them, so without measure disordered, that I think myself in hell till time come that I must go to Master Aylmer, who teacheth me so gently, so pleasantly, with such fair allurements to learning, that I think all the time nothing whilst I am with him. And when I am called from him, I fall on weeping because whatsoever I do else but learning is full of grief, trouble, fear, and whole misliking unto me. And thus my book hath been so much pleasure, and bringeth daily to me more pleasure and more, that in respect of it all other pleasures in very deed be but trifles and troubles unto me." I remember this talk gladly, both because it is so worthy of memory and because also it was the last talk I ever had, and the last time that I ever saw that noble and worthy lady. (Roger Ascham, *The Schoolmaster*)

ANSWER KEY

True-False Questions

1. F   2. F   3. T   4. F   5. T   6. T   7. F   8. T   9. T   10. F   11. T   12. F
13. T   14. T   15. F

Completion Questions

1. writing   2. correct   3. readers   4. audience   5. style   6. explains a topic
7. tells a story   8. explains   9. Effective   10. subject   11. active, passive
12. you   13. punctuation   14. semicolon   15. adverb

Multiple-Choice Questions

1. d   2. a   3. a   4. c   5. b   6. d   7. b   8. c   9. d   10. a

Further Exercises

1. The style is more formal than is common today, marked by long sentences and parallel structure. However, this passage is still very accessible.

2. The style is very formal, with elevated diction, archaic usages, and long sentences.

CHAPTER 13

Diction and Conciseness

Y ou should read this chapter if you need to review or learn about

Do I Need
to Read
This Chapter?

➡ Understanding the levels of diction

➡ Eliminating redundancy

➡ Making your sentences more concise and effective

Get Started

Here, you'll first explore *diction*, a writer's choice of words. Then you will learn how to eliminate unnecessary words from your writing to create a concise style. Understanding diction and conciseness will help you achieve a more effective writing style.

What is Diction?

- "When, in the course of human events, it becomes necessary for one people to dissolve the political bands which have connected them with another, and to assume, among the Powers of the earth, the separate and equal station to which the Laws of Nature and Nature's God entitle them, a decent respect to the opinions of mankind requires that they should declare the causes which impel them to the separation."

- "Get outta my way, bimbo!"

You likely recognize the first example: It's the opening of "The Declaration of Independence." The second example? It was yelled at me when a fellow driver decided that I wasn't driving fast enough (and I drive plenty fast!).

These two selections are very different because of their words. *Diction* is a writer's choice of words. Your diction affects the clarity and impact of your message. Therefore, the diction you want in a specific writing situation depends on context: your audience, purpose, and tone.

Levels of Diction

Diction is measured from *formal* to *informal* language usage. *Formal diction* is marked by multisyllable words, long sentences, and a formal tone; *informal diction* includes shorter words and sentences and a less formal tone. Neither level of diction (or any levels in between) is "good" or "bad"; rather, each is appropriate in different writing situations. The following chart shows the levels of diction and when each is used.

Formal Diction	Less Formal Diction	Informal Diction
Multisyllable words	Educated language	Everyday words
Legal documents	Job application letters	Popular magazine articles
Technical reports	Resumes	Notes to friends
Scientific articles	Sales and marketing letters	Everyday e-mail

Let's explore diction in greater detail.

1. Elevated diction

   The most elevated level of diction has abstract language, a serious tone, few personal references, few contractions, and considerable distance implied between reader and writer. It's used for the most formal documents such as stock offerings, land deeds, formal sermons, and technical articles.

   The following selection is from Jonathan Edwards' famous sermon "Sinners in the Hands of an Angry God," delivered in the early eighteenth century. As you read it, notice that the words are part of an educated person's vocabulary. Examples of *elevated diction* include *wrath* (great anger), *inconceivable* (cannot be imagined), and *abhor* (detest).

Notice also the great many *figures of speech,* such as the two imaginative comparisons. The first, a metaphor, compares God's anger to a bow and arrow: "The bow of God's wrath is bent, and the arrow made ready on the string, and justice bends the arrow at your heart and strains the bow. . . ." The second, a simile, compares humans to spiders: "The God that holds you over the pit of hell much as one holds a spider or some loathsome insect . . ."

> The wrath of God is like great waters that are dammed for the present; they increase more and more and rise higher and higher, till an outlet is given; and the longer the stream is stopped, the more rapid and mighty is its course when once it is let loose. 'Tis true that judgment against your evil work has not been executed hitherto; the floods of God's vengeance have been withheld; but your guilt in the meantime is constantly increasing, and you are every day treasuring up more wrath; the waters are continually rising and waxing more and more mighty; and there is nothing but the mere pleasure of God that holds the waters back, that are unwilling to be stopped, and press hard to go forward. If God should only withdraw his hand from the floodgate, it would immediately fly open, and the fiery floods of the fierceness and wrath of God would rush forth with inconceivable fury, and would come upon you with omnipotent power; and if your strength were ten thousand times greater than it is, yea, ten thousand times greater than the strength of the stoutest, sturdiest devil in hell, it would be nothing to withstand or endure it.
>
> The bow of God's wrath is bent, and the arrow made ready on the string, and justice bends the arrow at your heart and strains the bow, and it is nothing but the mere pleasure of God, and that of an angry God, without any promise or obligation at all, that keeps the arrow one moment from being made drunk with your blood.
>
> The God that holds you over the pit of hell much as one holds a spider or some loathsome insect over the fire, abhors you, and is dreadfully provoked; his wrath toward you burns like fire. . . .

2. Standard American English

The language used in most academic and professional writing is called "Edited American English" or "Standard Written English." It's the writing you find in magazines such as *Newsweek, US News and World Report,* and *The Atlantic.* Such language conforms to the widely established rules of grammar, sentence structure, usage, punctuation, and spelling that you've been learning in this book.

Here's an example of Standard American English from an article I wrote for a newspaper:

> When I was young, time seemed to stand still. But as I plunge kicking and screaming into my middle years, time compresses and I find myself thinking about eternity. No, not mortality, spirituality, or perfume; rather, I'm talking about the unique meaning "eternity" has for Long Islanders.
>
> To empty-nesters left contemplating the remains of an Easter feast once the guests have rolled out the door, eternity is two people and a ham. To my single female friends, eternity is waiting for Mr. Right to appear on their doorstep and in their arms. To a long-married man, eternity is shopping for shoes with his wife.
>
> To Long Islanders, however, eternity takes on a whole new meaning. My train-going friends claim that eternity is the Long Island Railroad loudspeaker squawking during rush hour, "LIRR delays through Jamaica, delays through Hicksville, delays on the Ronkonkoma branch." Why not just drive? You know the answer to that question if you've ever been westbound on the Southern State in the fall, as the sun sets on the highway and you're blinded for six straight miles. Traffic grinds to a

standstill as everyone fumbles with their sun visors and squints into their windshield. You know what eternity is when you travel from New York City to the Hamptons on a Friday night in August. They don't call it "Long" Island for nothing.

3. Colloquial language

Next comes *colloquial language,* the level of diction characteristic of casual conversation and informal writing. The following joke shows the difference between standard diction and colloquial language. Notice the contractions and the use of the word *buddies.*

> Three buddies die in a car crash and go to heaven for orientation. They're all asked, "When you're in your casket and friends and family are mourning you, what would you like to hear them say about you?"
>
> The first guy says, "I'd like to hear them say that I was a great doctor and a great family man."
>
> The second guy says, "I'd like to hear that I was a wonderful husband and teacher who made a huge difference in our children of tomorrow."
>
> The last guy replies, "I'd like to hear them say . . . '*Look, he's moving!*'"

4. Slang

Less formal than colloquial language is *slang,* coined words and phrases or new meanings for established terms. Some recent slang includes the words *dweeb, nerd, doofus.* Slang is fun, informal, and great for casual conversations with friends. Slang is never used in formal writing.

5. Vernacular

Vernacular is the ordinary language of a particular region, such as "pop" or "soda" for a carbonated beverage. *Dialect,* the language specific to a particular regional area, is a type of vernacular. It's different from slang because dialect reflects differences in regions and socioeconomic status. Like colloquial language and slang, vernacular and dialect are not appropriate for formal writing.

Here's how the novelist and humorist Mark Twain used vernacular and dialect to describe the people and events in the American West in the 1880s. This excerpt is from Twain's *Life on the Mississippi.*

> "Say, Jim, I'm a-goin' home for a few days."
>
> "What for?"
>
> "Well, I hain't b'en there for a right smart while and I'd like to see who things are comin' on."
>
> "How long are you going to be gone?"
>
> "'Bout two weeks."

Choosing the Appropriate Level of Diction

As you read earlier in this chapter, your choice of words depends on the context: your audience, purpose, and tone. Follow these guidelines as you select your level of diction:

1. Use words that are accurate, suitable, and familiar.
   - *Accurate* words say what you mean.
   - *Suitable* words convey your tone and fit with the other words in your writing.
   - *Familiar* words are easy to read and understand.

2. Choose the precise word you want.

    English is one of the richest languages in the world, one that offers many different ways to say the same thing. Select your words carefully to convey your thoughts vividly and precisely. Select words with the precise meanings you want. For example, *blissful, blithe, cheerful, contented, gay, joyful,* and *gladdened* all mean "happy"—yet each one conveys a different shade of meaning.

3. Use specific rather than general words.

    Specific words give your readers more vivid mental pictures than general words. Sometimes simple action verbs such as *run* and *go* will be appropriate to your subject, audience, and tone. Other times, however, you'll need more specific words to make your meaning clear.

4. Use words with the appropriate connotations.

    To be successful at choosing exact words for each particular context, you have to understand the *denotation* and *connotation* of words. Every word has a *denotation,* its explicit meaning. You can find the denotation of a word by looking it up in a dictionary. For example, if you look up the word *fat* in the dictionary, it will say, "having too much adipose tissue."

    Some words also have *connotations,* or emotional overtones. These connotations can be positive, negative, or neutral. For example, *fat* has a negative connotation in our fitness-obsessed society. Being sensitive to a word's denotation and connotation is essential for clear and effective writing. It can also help you use the right word and so avoid getting your nose punched out because you insulted someone. Finally, you can use these connotations to create—or defuse—an emotional response in your reader.

    Here are some additional examples of connotation and denotation:

Word	Positive Connotation	Negative Connotation
average	traditional	mediocre, passable
thrifty	economical	parsimonious, cheap, tightfisted
agreeable	amiable, easy-going	servile
caring	concerned	prying, meddlesome
daring	bold	defiant, reckless
deliberate	careful	slow
talkative	loquacious	verbose

Less Is More: Be Concise

The Elements of Style by William Strunk, Jr., and E. B. White is probably the most famous writing book of our time. This slender little volume contains this advice:

> Omit needless words.
>   Vigorous writing is concise. A sentence should contain no unnecessary words, a paragraph no unnecessary sentences, for the same reason that a drawing should have no unnecessary lines and a machine no unnecessary parts. (MacMillan, NY, 1959, p. 17)

You can't go wrong with this advice because an effective writing style shows an economy of language. When you omit needless words, you omit *redundancy*—the unnecessary repetition of words and ideas. Wordy writing forces your readers to clear away unnecessary words and phrases before they can understand your message.

Here are 10 redundant phrases and their concise revisions:

Redundant	Concise
at this point in time	now
fatally killed	killed
foreign imports	imports
kills bugs dead	kills bugs
live and breathe	live
most unique	unique
proceed ahead	proceed
revert back	revert
successfully escaped	escaped
true facts	facts (or truth)

I can't resist hammering the point home, so here are several more redundant phrases that make your writing flabby and verbose. As a result, be sure to cut them all! Your writing will be stronger and more vigorous, so your message will shine through clearly.

Redundant	Concise
at the present time	now
because of the fact that	because
completely surrounded on all sides	surrounded
due to the fact that	because
experience some discomfort	hurt
for the purpose of	for
free up some space	make room
in the event that	if
in order to utilize	to use
in order to	to
in view of the fact that	because
is an example of	is
it is believed by many that	many believe

Redundant	Concise
making an effort to	trying to
my personal physician	my doctor
reiterated over and over again	repeated
thunderstorm activity	thunderstorm
until such time as	until
weather event	snow (rain, etc.)

Conciseness describes writing that is direct and to the point. This is not to say that you have to pare away all description, figures of speech, and images. No. Rather, it *is* to say that wordy writing annoys your readers because it forces them to slash their way through your sentences before they can understand what you're saying. Writing concise and effective sentences requires far more effort than writing verbose and confusing sentences. Fortunately, your readers will appreciate your efforts.

Three Ways to Write Concise Sentences

Follow these rules to create succinct, effective sentences.

1. Eliminate unneeded words and phrases.
2. Combine sentences that repeat information.
3. Don't say the same thing twice.

Let's look at each of these rules more closely.

1. Eliminate unneeded words and phrases.

Filler words are empty words and phrases that add nothing to your sentences. Filler words are used to fill space and make writing sound "official." Unfortunately, many filler words have become so commonplace that we accept them as part of an effective style. Since they're not good writing, it's important to cut them from your documents. Since filler words are so annoying, think of your efforts to eliminate these space wasters as a public service in the name of good writing!

Filler words come in different parts of speech, as the following chart shows.

Part of Speech	Sample Filler Words		
Adjectives	main	excellent	good
	major	nice	
Adverbs	basically	central	major
	quite	really	very
	in fact	due to the fact that	in the process of

Part of Speech	Sample Filler Words		
Nouns	area	aspect	case
	character	element	factor
	field	kind	nature
	quality	scope	situation
	sort	thing	type

Here's how filler words look in context:

Wordy: Harris took a relaxing *type* of vacation.

Better: Harris took a relaxing vacation.

Wordy: His comment was *of an* offensive *nature*.

Better: His comment was offensive.

Wordy: Work crews arrived *for the purpose of* digging new power lines.

Better: Work crews arrived to dig new power lines.

Wordy: *Regardless of the fact that* a thunderstorm *activity* is not predicted for tomorrow, *in view of the fact that* it is cloudy, you should take your umbrella *anyway*.

Better: Although a thunderstorm is not predicted for tomorrow, because it is cloudy, you should take your umbrella.

Wordy: *In the event that we do have a weather event,* you will be prepared *in a very real sense.*

Better: If it does rain, you will be prepared.

Quick Tip

Eliminate these phrases as well:

the point I am trying to make	as a matter of fact	in a very real sense
in the case of that is to say	to get to the point	
what I mean to say in fact		

---

2. Combine sentences that repeat information.

 You also can combine sentences to achieve clarity. First, look for sentences that contain the same information or relate to the same ideas and so logically belong together. Then combine the related sentences. Finally, cut any words that just take up space and add nothing to the meaning. Here are some examples:

Wordy: Mr. Drucker gave his students the assignment of a math problem. The problem called for adding a series of numbers. The numbers contained real and imaginary integers.

Better: Mr. Drucker assigned his students a math problem that called for adding real and imaginary integers.

Wordy: There is strong evidence to suggest that there is only one difference between highly successful people and the rest of us. It is highly successful people who apply themselves with determination to a task.

Better: Evidence suggests that the only difference between highly successful people and the rest of us is their ability to apply themselves with determination to a task.

Quick Tip

Be careful not to change the meaning of a sentence when you combine it. If you trim too much, for instance, the meaning is likely to be altered.

3. Don't say the same thing twice.

Phrases such as "cover over," "circle around," and "square in shape" are redundant—they say the same thing twice. This is the redundancy problem you corrected in the beginning of this chapter.

Wordy: We hope *and trust* that you show insight *and vision* because it is fitting *and proper* that you do so.

Better: We hope that you show insight because it is fitting that you do so.

Wordy: I am *completely* upset by the extremely dangerous situation, and, *in light* of the fact that I think this is basically a terrible tragedy, I am not sure what the *eventual* outcome will be.

Better: I am upset by the dangerous situation; since this is a tragedy, I am not sure what the outcome will be.

Wordy: We watched the *big,* massive, *dark* black cloud rising *up* from the *level* prairie and covering *over* the sun.

Better: We watched the massive black cloud rising from the prairie and covering the sun.

Wordy: The package, rectangular *in shape,* was on the counter.

Better: The rectangular package was on the counter.

✔ *Diction* is word choice.

✔ Select words that suit your topic, purpose, and audience.

✔ *Redundancy* is unnecessary repetition of words and ideas. Eliminate unnecessary words and phrases to make your writing clearer and more vigorous.

QUESTIONS

True-False Questions

1. Neither formal nor informal diction (or any levels in between) is "good" or "bad"; rather, each is appropriate in different writing situations.

2. *Colloquial language* is the level of diction characteristic of casual conversation and informal writing.

3. More formal than colloquial language is *slang,* coined words and phrases or new meanings for established terms.

4. Like colloquial language and slang, *vernacular* and *dialect* are very appropriate for formal writing.

5. *Familiar* words are easy to read and understand, which makes them a good choice for most everyday writing that you do.

6. Use *general* rather than *specific* words to convey your meaning accurately.

7. Some words also have *connotations,* or emotional overtones.

8. A word's connotations can be positive but are rarely negative or neutral.

9. As a general rule, effective writing style shows an economy of language.

10. The phrase "at this point in time" is redundant.

Completion Questions

Select the word that best completes each sentence.

1. (Conciseness, Diction) is a writer's choice of words.

2. Diction is measured from formal to (informal, academic) language usage.

3. Legal documents are an example of (formal diction, informal diction).

4. (Resumes, Notes to friends) are usually written with informal diction.

5. The language standards used in most academic and professional writing is called "Edited American English" or ("Standard Written English," "Vernacular").

6. (Formal diction, Slang) is fun, informal, and great for casual conversations with friends, but it is never used in formal writing.

7. (Vernacular, Connotation) is the ordinary language of a particular region, such as *grinder, sub,* or *hero* for an oversized sandwich.

8. (Dialect, Denotation), the language specific to a particular regional area, is a type of vernacular.

9. Use words that are accurate, suitable, and (fancy, familiar).

10. Every word has a (connotation, denotation), its explicit meaning that can be found in a dictionary.

11. (Connotation, Redundancy) is the unnecessary repetition of words and ideas, when a writer says the same thing over and over in different words.

12. (Denotation, Filler words) are empty words and phrases that add nothing to your writing.

Multiple-Choice Questions

Choose the best answer to each question.

1. The diction you want in a specific writing situation depends on all the following *except*
   - (a) Your audience
   - (b) Your mood
   - (c) Your purpose
   - (d) The context of your message

2. In general, *formal diction* is characterized by all the following *except*
   - (a) Short, crisp sentences
   - (b) Multisyllable words
   - (c) Long sentences
   - (d) A formal tone

3. In general, *informal diction* is characterized by all the following *except*
   - (a) Shorter, more familiar words
   - (b) A less formal tone
   - (c) A greater awareness of audience
   - (d) Shorter sentences

4. Which of the following documents is usually written with formal diction?
   - (a) Job application letters
   - (b) Everyday e-mail
   - (c) Scientific articles
   - (d) Popular magazine articles

5. Which word has a negative connotation?
   - (a) Persistent
   - (b) Resolute

    (c) Steadfast

    (d) Stubborn

6. Which word has a positive connotation?

    (a) Arrogant

    (b) Proud

    (c) Egotistical

    (d) Overbearing

7. Which word has a denotation but no connotation?

    (a) House

    (b) Apathetic

    (c) Peculiar

    (d) Shrewd

8. Which word has the same connotation as *timid?*

    (a) Fainthearted

    (b) Cowardly

    (c) Shy

    (d) Fearful

9. Which is the best revision of the following wordy sentence?
Basically, the English language is so very difficult to learn.

    (a) English is very difficult to learn basically.

    (b) English is very difficult to learn.

    (c) English is basically very difficult to learn.

    (d) The English language is very difficult to learn.

10. Which is the best revision of the following wordy sentence?
It seems that the library board will meet tomorrow, as a matter of fact.

    (a) As a matter of fact, the library board will meet tomorrow.

    (b) In fact, the library board will meet tomorrow.

    (c) It is apparent that the library board will meet tomorrow.

    (d) The library board will meet tomorrow.

11. Which is the best revision of the following wordy sentence?
Intelligent consumers don't let fashion gurus dictate their purchases. These fashion gurus want women to spend money on trendy garments. Trendy garments are poor investments in the long run.

    (a) Intelligent consumers don't let fashion gurus dictate their purchases because these fashion gurus want women to spend money on trendy garments, but trendy garments are poor investments in the long run.

    (b) Since fashion gurus want women to spend money on trendy garments, intelligent consumers don't let fashion gurus dictate their purchases; trendy garments are poor investments in the long run.

    (c)   Intelligent women don't let fashion gurus persuade them to spend money on trendy garments since, in the long run, trendy garments that are poor investments.

    (d)   Intelligent women don't let fashion gurus persuade them to spend money on trendy garments that are poor investments.

12. Which is the best revision of the following wordy sentence?
Today's women have a mind of their own when it comes to clothing. They don't rely on advice from talk shows. They don't rely on advice from books, either. Finally, they don't depend on the dictates of fashion magazines.

    (a)   Women today have a mind of their own when it comes to clothing, so they don't rely on advice from talk shows and they don't rely on advice from books and they don't depend on the dictates of fashion magazines.

    (b)   Women today know a lot about clothing.

    (c)   Today's women, who have a mind of their own when it comes to clothing, don't rely on advice from talk shows or books. They don't even take advice from fashion magazines.

    (d)   Today's women, who have a mind of their own when it comes to clothing, don't rely on advice from talk shows, books, or fashion magazines.

13. What's the best simplification of the following redundant phrase: "at this point in time"?

    (a)   Now

    (b)   Never never land

    (c)   Never ever

    (d)   Later

14. What is the problem with the phrase "true facts"?

    (a)   Only some facts are true.

    (b)   All facts are true; otherwise, they wouldn't be facts.

    (c)   It has a negative connotation.

    (d)   It does not have a denotation.

15. Follow all the rules below to create succinct, effective sentences *except*

    (a)   Eliminate unneeded words and phrases.

    (b)   Combine sentences that repeat information.

    (c)   Write as you speak.

    (d)   Don't say the same thing twice.

ANSWER KEY

True-False Questions

       1. T   2. T   3. F   4. F   5. T   6. F   7. T   8. F   9. T   10. T

Completion Questions

1. Diction   2. informal   3. formal diction   4. Notes to friends
5. Standard Written English   6. Slang   7. Vernacular   8. Dialect   9. familiar
10. denotation   11. Redundancy   12. Filler words

Multiple-Choice Questions

1. b   2. a   3. c   4. c   5. d   6. b   7. a   8. c   9. b   10. d   11. d   12. d
13. a   14. b   15. c

CHAPTER 14

Words and Expressions to Avoid

You should read this chapter if you need to review or learn about

Do I Need to Read This Chapter?

➡️ Avoiding biased language

➡️ Rewriting clichés

➡️ Replacing overblown words with direct expressions

Get Started

Every time you write, you want to get your message across clearly. The words you choose enable you to achieve your purpose. In this chapter, you'll learn how to avoid biased language, replace overworked expressions with fresh ones, and replace stuffy language with clear speech. This will help you create an honest, direct, and effective writing style.

Use Nonbiased Language

Language is a powerful tool: We use it deliberately to shape our thoughts and experiences, yet our language can shape us. You wouldn't discriminate against people based on their race, disability, or age—so neither should your words. Therefore, always use *bias-free language.* This type of language uses words and phrases that don't discriminate on the basis of gender, physical condition, age, race, gender, or any other quality. That way, your readers will be able to concentrate on *what* you say rather than on *how* you say it.

1. Refer to a group by the term it prefers.

   Language changes, so stay on the cutting edge. For example, a hundred years ago, black people were called *colored.* Fifty years later, the term *Negro* was used. Today, the preferred terms are *African American* and *black.* Here are some other changes to know:

   - *Asian* is preferred over *Oriental.*
   - *Inuit* is preferred over *Eskimo.*
   - *Latino* is the preferred designation for males with Central and Latin American backgrounds.
   - *Latina* is the preferred designation for females with Central and Latin American backgrounds.
   - Only give someone's race if it is relevant to your narrative. Further, if you do mention one person's race, be sure to mention everyone else's.

Quick Tip

Members of the same ethnic or religious group sometimes call each other by denigrating racial terms. Don't go there.

---

2. Focus on people, not their conditions.

   Actor Lou Ferrigno ("The Incredible Hulk") is 60 percent deaf. President Franklin Delano Roosevelt was paralyzed from the waist down as a result of polio. Singer Neil Young and actor Danny Glover have epilepsy. Singer Ray Charles is blind. Actor Tom Cruise and actor-singer Cher have dyslexia, a processing disorder that impedes reading.

   People with disabilities can be defined broadly as those with limitations in human actions or activities due to physical, emotional, or mental impairments. According to the U.S. Census Bureau, about 49 million Americans have a disability; the number with a severe disability is 24.1 million. Expect the number to increase as the population ages. Therefore, it is important to know the accepted ways of referring to people with illnesses.

Biased:	the deaf
Nonbiased:	people with hearing impairments
Biased:	AIDS patients
Nonbiased:	people being treated for AIDS

Biased:	the mentally retarded
Nonbiased:	people with mental retardation
Biased:	abnormal, afflicted, struck down
Nonbiased:	atypical

3. Avoid language that discriminates against older people.

Biased:	old people, geezers, aged
Nonbiased:	Senior citizen, mature person

4. Avoid sexist language.

   "Hey, babe, you are one foxy chick."

   "He has such a male ego!"

We all know that such blatant sexist language and attitudes aren't acceptable in today's world. But sexist language can be much less obvious—and every bit as offensive.

Sexist language assigns qualities to people on the basis of their gender. It reflects prejudiced attitudes and stereotypical thinking about the sex roles and traits of both men and women and so discriminates against people by limiting what they can do.

Further, the law is increasingly intolerant of biased documents and hostile work environments. Since federal law forbids discrimination on the basis of gender, people writing *anything*—but especially policy statements, grant proposals, or any other official documents—must be very careful not to use any language that could be considered discriminatory. Otherwise, they're just looking for a lawsuit.

Nonsexist language treats both sexes neutrally. It does not make assumptions about the proper gender for a job, nor does it assume that men take precedence over women. Here are some guidelines to help you use nonsexist language when you write and speak.

- Avoid using *man, he,* or *him* to refer to both men and women.

Sexist:	A person could lose *his* way in this huge store.
Nonbiased:	A person could get lost in this huge store.

or

   You could lose your way in this huge store.

- Avoid expressions that exclude one sex. Here are some of the most offensive examples and acceptable alternatives:

Sexist	Nonbiased
chairman	chair, moderator
common man	average person
congressman	senator, representative
female intuition	intuition
female lawyer	lawyer
fireman	firefighter

Continues

Sexist	Nonbiased
foreman	supervisor
male ego	ego
male nurse	nurse
mankind	humanity, people
old wives' tale	superstition
policeman	police officer
postman	postal carrier, letter carrier
stewardess	flight attendant
waitress	server
workman	worker, employee, or the specific job title

Quick Tip

Watch for phrases that suggest women and men behave in stereotypical ways, such as "cries like a woman," "thinks like a man," "man's work," "rowdy boys." Expunge such phrases from your writing and speech.

- Use the correct courtesy title.

  Use *Mr.* for men and *Ms.* for women, with these two exceptions: In a business setting, professional titles take precedence over Mr. and Ms. For example, on the job, I am referred to as *Dr.* Rozakis rather than *Ms.* Rozakis.

- Always use the title the person prefers.

  Some women prefer *Miss* to *Ms.* If you are not sure what courtesy title to use, check in a company directory or on previous correspondence to see how the person prefers to be addressed. Also pay attention to the way people introduce themselves.

- Use plural pronouns and nouns whenever possible.

  Sexist: A good reporter needs to verify *her* sources.

  Nonbiased: Good reporters need to verify *their* sources.

Replace Clichés with Fresh Expressions

As you read this section, be sure to roll out the red carpet, keep your eyes peeled, your fingers crossed, and your head above water and you may be able to keep up with the Joneses.

But that's only if you're on the ball, beam, go, level, and up-and-up, rather than on the fly, fence, ropes, rocks, or lam. Or you can just go fry an egg.

The previous paragraph was chock-full of *clichés,* descriptive phrases that have lost their effectiveness through overuse. If you have heard the same words and phrases over and over, so has your reader. Replace clichés with fresh, new descriptions. If you can't think of a way to rewrite the phrase to make it new, delete it completely.

Cliché	Meaning
clean as a hound's tooth	very clean
cry uncle	give up
get cold feet	afraid to proceed
make your hair stand on end	terrified
on the carpet	reprimanded
on the fritz	broken
on the lam	fleeing
on the make	eager for financial or sexual gain
rain or shine	regardless
soft as silk	soft

Remember, if you have a tough row to hoe, be a tough nut to crack and tough it out. Truth will win out and you can turn over a new leaf, turn the tables, other cheek, or the corner. Under a cloud? Not up to par, scratch, or snuff? Use your head; it's all water over the dam. After all: the world is your oyster; you can bet your bottom dollar!

Avoid Empty Language

When's the last time someone tried to sell you an "underground condominium"? It's the newest term for a grave. See any "personal manual data bases" being hawked on the home shopping network? They're what we used to call calendars.

These phrases are artificial, evasive language. Each one pretends to communicate but really doesn't. It is language that makes the bad seem good, the negative appear positive, the unpleasant become pleasant. It shifts responsibility and deliberately aims to distort and deceive.

Phrase	Meaning
greenmail	economic blackmail
involuntarily leisured	fired
mechanically separated meat	salvaged meat
nonpositively terminated	fired
outplaced	fired
revenue enhancement	tax increase
sea legs	pressed seafood
takeover artists	corporate raiders
unauthorized withdrawal	robbery
vertically challenged	a short person

Here are some additional examples of evasive language:

When writers use this kind of language, they hide the truth. Always use language truthfully.

1. Avoid inflated language.
   Inflated language makes the ordinary seem extraordinary.
   > "automotive internists" for car mechanics
   > "vertical transportation corps" for elevator operators

   Now, I'm all for giving someone praise (and even a fancy job title), but inflated language is fundamentally dishonest because it manipulates the truth. Therefore, write and speak clearly and directly.

2. Use euphemisms with care.
   What do all the following expressions have in common?
   - She's between jobs.
   - He has to see a man about a horse.
   - He cashed in his chips.
   - She's pushing up daisies.
   - She's a woman of a certain age.

   These sentences are all *euphemisms,* inoffensive or positive words or phrases used to avoid a harsh reality. Euphemisms are a type of evasive language because they cloud the truth. You find them in all potentially embarrassing situations, such as losing a job, bathroom activities, dying, nudity, body parts, sex, and aging.
   - Avoid euphemisms if they obscure your meaning. Most of the time, euphemisms drain meaning from truthful writing. As a result, they can make it difficult for your readers and listeners to understand your meaning.
   - Use euphemisms to spare someone's feelings, especially in delicate situations. You *should* use euphemisms when you are trying to spare someone's feelings or out of concern for a recognized social custom, as when you say, "I am sorry your sister passed away" rather than "I am sorry your sister died."

3. Avoid bureaucratic language.

Bureaucratic language is wordy and unnecessarily complex. As a result, it becomes meaningless because it is evasive and wordy.

Original: The internal memorandum previously circulated should be ignored and disregarded and instead replaced by the internal memorandum sent before the previous one was sent. The memorandum presently at the current time being held by the appropriate personnel should be combined with the previous one to call attention to the fact that the previous one should be ignored by the reader.

Revision: Replace the first memorandum you received with the one that followed it. Please attach this notice to the canceled version.

Use the following checklist to identify empty language in all its forms. As you reread your own writing to eliminate empty language, ask yourself these questions:

- What do my words mean?
- To whom is the remark addressed?
- Under what conditions is the remark being made?
- What is my intent?
- What is the result of the remarks?
- Which words will help me express my ideas most clearly and directly?

George Orwell on Style

"George Orwell" was the pen name of Eric Blair, one of the most brilliant English stylists ever. In his landmark essay "Politics and the English Language," Orwell wrote, "Modern English prose . . . consists less and less of words chosen for the sake of their meaning, and more and more of phrases tacked together like the sections of a prefabricated henhouse." He concluded: "The great enemy of clear language is insincerity. When there is a gap between one's real and one's declared aims, one turns as it were instinctively to long words and exhausted idioms, like a cuttlefish squirting out ink."

But Orwell didn't just complain. Fortunately, he suggested a number of remedies. His guidelines have become the classic yardstick for a strong and effective writing style.

1. Never use a metaphor, simile, or other figure of speech which you are used to seeing in print.
   (This is covered in this chapter in the section Replace Clichés with Fresh Expressions.)

2. Never use a long word where a short one will do.
   (This is covered in this chapter in the section Avoid Empty Language.)

3. If it is possible to cut a word out, always cut it out.
   (This is covered in Chapter 13 in the sections Less is More: Be Concise and Three Ways to Write Concise Sentences.)

4. Never use the passive voice when you can use the active.
   (This is covered in Chapter 3 in the section Active and Passive Voice.)

5. Never use a foreign phrase, a scientific word, or a jargon word if you can think of an every-day English equivalent.
(This is covered in this chapter in the section Avoid Empty Language.)

6. Break any of these rules sooner than say anything outright barbarous.

Quick Tip

Steer clear of slanted language—emotionally loaded words and phrases designed to inflame readers. Describing a lab experiment as "viciously maiming helpless rats" is an example of slanted language. At its most offensive, slanted language descends into propaganda; at its best, slanted language merely offends readers.

✔ Use bias-free language.

✔ Replace clichés with fresh expressions.

✔ Avoid empty language.

✔ Write simply and directly.

QUESTIONS

True-False Questions

1. Always use bias-free language, language that uses words and phrases that don't discriminate on the basis of gender, physical condition, age, race, gender, or any other quality.

2. Today, the term *Oriental* is preferred over *Asian*.

3. Likewise, *Latina* is the preferred designation for males with Central and Latin American backgrounds.

4. Only give someone's race if it is relevant to your narrative. Further, if you do mention one person's race, be sure to mention everyone else's.

5. The nonbiased term is "the deaf"; the biased term is "people with hearing impairments."

6. Sexist language assigns qualities to people on the basis of their gender.

7. Sexist language discriminates only against women, not men.

8. Nonsexist language treats both sexes neutrally.

9. Avoid using *man, he,* or *him* to refer to both men and women.

10. In a business setting, professional titles do not take precedence over *Mr.* and *Ms.*

11. To make your language nonbiased, use plural pronouns and nouns whenever possible.

12. If you want your documents to sound important, use a little inflated language, words and expressions that make the ordinary seem extraordinary.

13. Avoid euphemisms if they obscure your meaning.

14. Use euphemisms to spare someone's feelings, especially in delicate situations.

15. *Clichés* are wordy and unnecessarily complex. As a result, clichés become meaningless because they are evasive and wordy.

Completion Questions

Rewrite each sentence to remove the bias.

1. We need more manpower.

2. Mrs. Yu looks remarkably good for her age.

3. These stockings are available in black, suntan, and flesh color.

4. I see that Marci forgot to bring her lunch. She's acting a little blonde today.

5. Mrs. Clinton and George W. Bush met to discuss strategy.

6. Pat really went on the warpath when her son stayed out past his curfew.

7. The club now admits women and other minorities.

8. Women can leave their children at the daycare center.

9. Win a fabulous vacation: a day at the spa for her and 18 holes of golf for him.

10. We welcomed all guests, their wives, and their children.

11. I completely forgot where I put the package; I must be having a senior moment.

12. Studying the techniques by which an actor achieved his success can help other actors succeed.

13. Each doctor should send one of his nurses to the seminar.

14. If you use a technical word that he won't understand, explain it to him.

15. Each department head should report her progress by May 1.

Multiple-Choice Questions

Choose the best answer to each question.

1. Which of the following terms is considered sexist today?
    (a) Senator
    (b) Representative
    (c) Average person
    (d) Mankind

2. Today, all the following terms are considered biased *except*

   (a) Fireman

   (b) Policeman

   (c) Humanity

   (d) Female lawyer

3. A cliché is

   (a) An overused expression, often a metaphor or simile

   (b) A fresh, vivid description

   (c) Rarely found in everyday speech and writing

   (d) Inflated language that contains many unnecessary words

4. All the following expressions are considered clichés *except*

   (a) As fresh as a daisy

   (b) A torrid thunderstorm

   (c) Right as rain

   (d) Sick as a dog

5. All the following expressions are examples of evasive, dishonest language *except*

   (a) Made redundant

   (b) Fresh bread

   (c) Laid off

   (d) Involuntarily leisured

6. The phrase "automotive internists" for car mechanics is an example of

   (a) A simile

   (b) Inflated language

   (c) A metaphor

   (d) A cliché

7. *Euphemisms* are best defined as

   (a) Words and phrases that don't discriminate on the basis of gender, physical condition, age, race, gender, or any other quality

   (b) Overused words and phrases

   (c) Inflated language that contains many unnecessary words

   (d) Inoffensive or positive words or phrases used to avoid a harsh reality

8. Language that is wordy and unnecessarily complex is often called

   (a) Euphemisms

   (b) Clichés

   (c) Bureaucratic language

   (d) Sexist

9. George Orwell gave writers all the following advice *except*

   (a) If it is possible to cut a word out, always cut it out.

   (b) Never use a long word where a short one will do.

    (c) Never use a metaphor, simile, or other figure of speech which you are used to seeing in print.

    (d) Never use the active voice when you can use the passive voice.

10. All the following advice about writing style is valid *except*

    (a) Write as you speak.

    (b) Write simply, clearly, and directly.

    (c) Suit your words to your purpose, audience, and topic.

    (d) Use fresh and descriptive words and expressions.

Further Exercises

Briefly describe the style of each of the following selections, identifying the purpose and audience. Then decide which style is closest to your own and why. If you wish to change your writing style, which essay is closest to the style you want to adopt?

1. When a writer calls his work a Romance, it need hardly be observed that he wishes to claim a certain latitude, both to its fashion and material, which he would not have felt himself entitled to assume, had he professed to be writing a Novel. The latter form of composition is presumed to aim at a very minute fidelity, not merely to the possible, but to the probable and ordinary course of man's experience. The former—while, as a work of art, it must rigidly subject itself to laws, and while it sins unpardonably, so far as it may swerve aside from the truth of the human heart—has fairly a right to present that truth under the circumstances, to a great extent, of the writer's own choosing or creation. If he think fit, also, he may so manage his atmospherical medium as to bring out or mellow the lights and deepen and enrich the shadows of the picture. He will be wise, no doubt, to make a very moderate use of the privileges here stated, and, especially, to mingle the Marvelous rather as a slight, delicate, and evanescent flavor, than as any portion of the actual substance of the dish offered to the public. (Nathaniel Hawthorne)

2. And so the reliance on property, including the reliance on governments which protect it, is the want of self-reliance. Men have looked away from themselves and at things so long that they have come to esteem the religious, learned and civil institutions as guards of property, and they deprecate assaults on these, because they feel them to be assaults on property. They measure their esteem of each other by what each has, and not by what each is. But a cultivated man becomes ashamed of his property, out of new respect for his nature. Especially he hates what he has if he sees that it is accidental—came to him by inheritance, or gift, or crime; then he feels that it is not having; it does not belong to him, has no root in him and merely lies there because no revolution or no robber takes it away. But that which a man is, does always by necessity acquire; and what the man acquires, is living property, which does not wait the beck of rulers, or mobs, or revolutions, or fire, or storm, or bankruptcies, but perpetually renews itself wherever the man breathes. "Thy lot or portion of life," said the Caliph Ali, "is seeking after thee; therefore be at rest from seeking after it." Our dependence on these foreign goods leads us to our slavish respect for numbers. The political parties meet in numerous conventions; the greater the concourse and with each new uproar of announcement, The delegation from Essex! The Democrats from New Hampshire! The Whigs of Maine! The young

patriot feels himself stronger than before by a new thousand of eyes and arms. In like manner the reformers summon conventions and vote and resolve in multitude. Not so, O friends! Will the God deign to enter and inhabit you, but by a method precisely the reverse. It is only as a man puts off all foreign support and stands alone that I see him to be strong and to prevail. He is weaker by every recruit to his banner. Is not a man better than a town? He who knows that power is inborn, that he is weak because he has looked for good out of him and elsewhere, and, so perceiving, throws himself unhesitatingly on his thought, instantly fights himself, stands in the erect position, commands his limbs, works miracles; just as a man who stands on his feet is stronger than a man who stands on his head. (Ralph Waldo Emerson)

3. The film industry changed from silent films to the "talkies" in the late 1920s, after the success in 1927 of *The Jazz Singer.* Mickey Mouse was one of the few "stars" who made a smooth transition from silent films to talkies. Mickey made his first cartoon with sound in November 1928. The cartoon was called *Steamboat Willie.* Walt Disney (1901–1966) drew Mickey as well as used his own voice for Mickey's high-pitched tones. Within a year, hundreds of Mickey Mouse clubs had sprung up all across the United States. By 1931, more than a million people belong to a Mickey Mouse club. The phenomenon was not confined to America. In London, Madame Tussaud's famous wax museum placed a wax figure of Mickey alongside its statues of other famous film stars. In 1933, according to Disney Studios, Mickey received 800,000 fan letters—an average of more than 2,000 letters a day. This was the same number of letters sent to the top human stars of the day such as Douglas Fairbanks, Senior. To date, no "star" has ever received as much fan mail as Mickey Mouse. (Laurie Rozakis)

4. While there are currently no societies where we can observe creolization occurring with a spoken language, we can observe the creolization of sign languages for the deaf. Since 1979, in Nicaragua, children at schools for the deaf have essentially formed a pidgin. None of them had a real signing system, so they pooled their collections of makeshift gestures into what is now called the Lenguaje de Signos Nicaragüense (LSN). Like any spoken pidgin, LSN is a collection of jargon that has no consistent grammar, and everyone who uses it uses it differently.

When younger children joined the school, after LSN existed, they creolized it into what is called Idioma de Signos Nicaragüense (ISN). While LSN involves a lot of pantomime, ISN is much more stylized, fluid and compact. And children who use ISN all use it the same way—the children had created a standardized language without need for textbooks or grammar classes. Many grammatical devices, such as tenses and complex sentence structures, that didn't exist in LSN, were introduced by the children into ISN. (Charles Rozakis)

ANSWER KEY

True-False Questions

1. T   2. F   3. F   4. T   5. F   6. T   7. F   8. T   9. T   10. F   11. T   12. F
13. T   14. T   15. F

Completion Questions

Answers will vary; below are suggested responses.

1. We need more assistance.
2. Mrs. Yu looks remarkably good.
3. These stockings are available in black, suntan, and beige color.
4. I see that Marci forgot to bring her lunch. She's acting a little distracted today.
5. Hilary Clinton and George W. Bush (or Ms. Clinton and Mr. Bush) met to discuss strategy.
6. Pat became very angry when her son stayed out past his curfew.
7. The club no longer has restrictions on membership.
8. Parents can leave their children at the daycare center.
9. Win a fabulous vacation, including a day at the spa and 18 holes of golf.
10. We welcomed all guests and their children.
11. I completely forgot where I put the package; I must be getting forgetful.
12. Studying the techniques by which actors achieved success can help other actors succeed.
13. All doctors should send one of their nurses to the seminar.
14. If you use a technical word that a person won't understand, explain it to the person.
15. Each department head should report their department's progress by May 1.

Multiple-Choice Questions

1. d　2. c　3. a　4. b　5. b　6. b　7. d　8. c　9. d　10. a

Further Exercises

1. This essay, aimed at an educated readership, has an elevated style and intends to instruct. The style is characterized by long sentences, difficult words, and fresh language.
2. This essay, aimed at an educated readership, also has an elevated style and intends to instruct. The style is characterized by long sentences, difficult words, and fresh language.
3. This passage, aimed at an everyday audience (such as magazine readers), has a less-elevated style. It is characterized by short sentences, description, and a light tone.
4. This passage, part of a school paper, is aimed at a professor. It is marked by technical terms and great specific details.

Index

Index